CHINA

CHINA

IAN WESTWELL

CHARTWELL
BOOKS, INC.

This edition published in 2007 by

CHARTWELL BOOKS, INC.
A Division of
BOOK SALES, INC.
114 Northfield Avenue
Edison, New Jersey 08837

ISBN 13: 978-0-7858-2374-2
ISBN 10: 0-7858-2374-3

© 2007 Compendium Publishing Ltd
43 Frith Street, London, WC1V 4SA
United Kingdom

Project Manager: Stuart Booth
Designer: Danny Gillespie

Printed and bound in China

PAGE ONE: The characteristic karst limestone hills around Yangshuo,
intersected by the beautiful Li River in Guangxi province.

TITLE PAGE: Hilly fields of canola growing near the mountains of
Guizhou province.

RIGHT: A costumed, mask-changing dancer from the Wu Hou shrine's
traditional theater group of Chengdu in Sichuan province.

FAR RIGHT: Traditional dragons framing the Taiwanese capital's tower
which is known as Taipei 101 (see also page 209).

Contents

Introduction

Archeologists have found evidence of a sedentary agricultural community near modern-day Xian that dates back some 6000 years, as well evidence of what has been named Longshan culture near Shandong. The latter people seem to have developed metalworking and are believed to have laid the foundation for the Shang Dynasty, which flourished between 1700 BCE and 1100 BCE. The Shang settled much of northern China with their capital at Anyang and their society consisted of a religious leader, who ruled over a society that was divided between officials, soldiers, metalworker, and peasants.

The next dynasty to develop was the Zhou, which emerged around 1100 BCE and survived until 221 BCE. Their homeland lay in what is now Shaanxi Province in central China; but they pushed out as far as Beijing and also south to the valley of the Chang Jiang. The Zhou Dynasty is usually divided into two eras: that of the Western Zhou, who ruled from 1100 to 771 BCE and made Hao, near Xian, their capital; and the Eastern Zhou (1100 to 221 BCE), who ruled from Luoyang. The Zhou's realm was divided into a number of principalities that were dominated by governors, who exercised power from walled cities. They were in frequent conflict with each other, especially in the latter 250 years or so of the dynasty–the so-called "Warring States period".

That period of conflict finally came to an end in 221 BCE, when the Qin conquered the last of the Warring States after a 35-year campaign. Qin Shi Huang became the first Qin emperor and set out to extent his rule into Korea and Vietnam through. Inevitably, he did this by military force but he also began the vast construction project that, ultimately, produced the Great Wall. He laid the foundations for a strong and united empire; but his successor was far too weak and the dynasty was overthrown in 207 BCE by Liu Bang and who established the Han Dynasty.

The Han ruled until 220 CE and extended the empire by annexing neighboring states. The dynasty is divided into three eras: the Western Han (206 BCE to 9 CE), who made Xian their capital; the Xin (9 to 23 CE), in which Wang Mang briefly held power; and the Eastern Han (24 to 220 CE).

The Han sought contact with China's neighbors, but with mixed results. Some of these links led to the development of more trading routes, most notably the Silk Road; but on other occasions they led to war. Eventually, the Han collapsed and were followed by a long era of disunity and violence. This is commonly split into three major periods; the Three Kingdoms (220–280), the Jin (264–420), and the Southern and North Dynasties (420–589). The various outbreaks of warfare that typified these years led to significant split between the north and south of the country. Non-Chinese peoples ruled the Chinese living in the north, who decided to head south in order to escape persecution, thereby spreading their Chinese culture into new regions as it died out simultaneously in the north.

The short-lived Sui Dynasty (581–618) brought a measure of stability to China. But real progress was made only after their last ruler, Sui Yangdi, was assassinated in 618. He was replaced by one of his senior commanders, Li Yuan, who founded the Tang Dynasty and spent the next decade ruthlessly removing any potential rivals. The Tang held power until the year 907 and their rule is now generally regarded as something of a "golden age". They began by reorganizing China in order to prevent the outbreak of the type of unrest that had split the state apart for so many years.

In fact, the Tang dynasty's rule was briefly interrupted briefly between 690 and 705, when Wu Zhao–the previous emperor's concubine–seized power. She remains the only female in Chinese history to officially have become head of state and was widely believed to have been excessively brutal in her rule. But under her leadership, the empire became larger than ever before and she also introduced a system wee officials were selected on merit rather than mere ranks. Wu was a strong supporter of Buddhism and this led to her downfall in 705, when she abdicated and was replaced by Xuan Zong.

External threats and internal divisions began to weaken the power of the Tang Dynasty from the eighth century onward due to external threats and internal divisions. Discontent with the regime eventually turned into the Huang Chao Rebellion (874 to 884) and to the fall in 907 of the Tang capital, Xian, that signaled the end of their rule.

A period of further instability, which is commonly divided between the time of the Five Dynasties and Ten Kingdoms (907 to 960) and the Liam (907 to 1125), ensued, but a greater measure of stability returned with the creation of the Song Dynasty in 960. This era is usually considered to have consisted of two periods, the Northern and Southern Song.

The former (960 to1127) controlled a smallish empire that was bordered by more powerful neighbors including the Liam. The Northern Song also faced threats from other nearby states, especially the Xi Xian on its northwest border but the Northern song capital at Knifing actually fell to the Urchin in 1126. The Northern Song fled to create a new capital at Hang Zhou and transformed themselves into the Southern Song (1127 to 1279), while the Jurchen established Jin Dynasty (1115 to 1234), making Kaifeng and then Beijing their capital. Although the Jin extracted tribute from the Song, the latter era was a time of considerable economic expansion that was matched by a flowering of the arts.

Both the Song and Jinn Dynasties came under threat after the great warlord Genghis Khan became the acknowledged and unchallenged leader of the Mongols in 1206. The Mongols had previously been unsuccessful in campaigning against Chin; but all that changed in 1211, when Genghis returned at the head of his might army. His forces broke through the Great Wall two years later and became masters of Beijing in 1215. Genghis, who died in 1227, was the founding father of the Mongol Empire but much work was also done by his successors. The Jin Dynasty was brought to its knees in 1234 and the Mongols took the Southern Song capital in 1276, dealing with their last pockets of resistance a mere three years later.

The grandson of Genghis, Kublai Khan, ruled over all China under the name of the Yuan Dynasty (1206–1368). His was the greatest empire the world had ever seen and its borders were opened to traders and missionaries from as far afield as Europe. The Mongols ruled over a highly stratified society. They largely held the top administrative positions themselves with their non-Chinese allies holding the lower grades. The system caused increasing resentment among the Chinese and the introduction of an examination system for entry into the bureaucracy did little to change matters as it was still seen to favor the Mongols and non-Chinese. Mongol rule over China was comparative brief, around 150 years, and their empire fell apart because of their biased political system and failure to control the economy.

Toward the end of their dynasty, the Yuan faced rebellions that they failed to crush despite the supposed military might. There were several groups involved in the uprising but the leader of one of them, Zhu Yuanzhang, became their chief and he reasserted Chinese rule in 1368, when the Ming Dynasty was founded. Zhu was a brutal man and frequently launched bloody

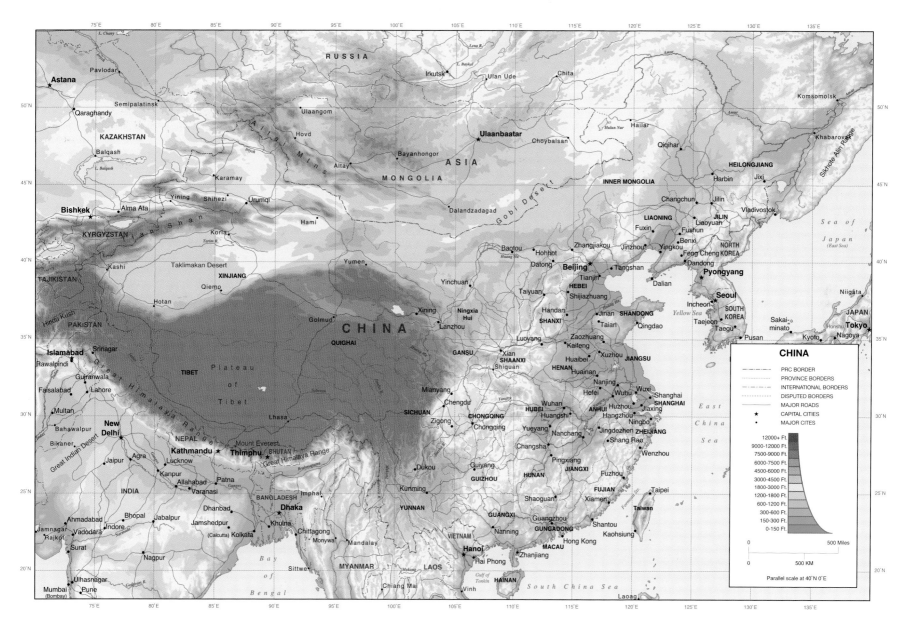

CHINA

PRC BORDER
PROVINCE BORDERS
INTERNATIONAL BORDERS
DISPUTED BORDERS
MAJOR ROADS
★ CAPITAL CITIES
• MAJOR CITES

12000+ Ft.
9000-12000 Ft.
7500-9000 Ft.
6000-7500 Ft.
4500-6000 Ft.
3000-4500 Ft.
1800-3000 Ft.
1200-1800 Ft.
600-1200 Ft.
300-600 Ft.
150-300 Ft.
0-150 Ft.

0   500 Miles

0   500 KM

Parallel scale at 40°N 0°E

LEFT: The Great Wall of China follows the natural contours of the Chinese landscape.

RIGHT: A mother and child from Tongren in the traditional Tibetan dress of southern Guizhou province.

assaults against those he thought to be his enemies but he also brought a measure of stability to China after the turmoil that had accompanied the collapse of the Yuan Dynasty.

The Ming established their first capital at Nanjing, but they gradually moved back to Beijing, the former Mongol capital, in the early part of the fifteenth century. The Ming greatly expanded and redeveloped their capital, especially under the reign of Yongle, who built much of the Forbidden City. The emperor was beset with problems at home, not least because he had actually grabbed power, and he strove for acceptance by embarking on a series of naval expeditions to establish links with other states.

Although the Ming had ousted the Mongol Yuan Dynasty, the latter were far from a spent force and in 1439 launched a raid into China that led to the capture of the emperor. He was eventually released after 12 months, but the traumatic event created a great sense of insecurity, especially along their northern border. The Ming extended and strengthened the Great Wall at great expense during the second half of the century to prevent further violent incursions but they were happy to allow foreign traders onto their soil.

The Ming Dynasty fell as a result of several factors. Firstly, there was a succession of weak emperors who failed to deal firmly with unrest and placed their own interests before those of the country. Then, floods and poor harvests in the north provoked uprisings, while the resurgent Jurchen people began to make damaging raids into the country.

The weakness of the Ming Dynasty was noted by the Manchu people across the northeastern border and they decided to take China by force. Initially, their efforts were frustrated by the Great Wall, but they gained entry after a Chinese general allowed them to enter–in the wholly mistaken belief that the Manchu would help to quash the various internal uprisings that were crippling the country. It was a fateful error. Beijing fell to one of the rebel leaders in 1644; but he held power for a mere 24 hours before being ousted by the Manchu.

 The Manchu named their dynasty Qing. It took the best part of 40 years of campaigning to stamp the last vestiges of support for the Ming; but thereafter, they ruled until the early twentieth century. The Qing set out to extend the country's borders and unite the various peoples found within them. They incorporated their own homeland of Manchuria into China and then took in the areas that were still controlled by the Mongols. Formosa (Taiwan) was captured in 1683 and Tibet made a Chinese colony in 1751. This territorial expansion, whist placing an ever-increasing burden on the country's finances, was matched by a rising birth rate–so much so that the Chinese population more than doubled to 350 million or so between the mid-seventeenth and the late eighteenth centuries.

Close attention was paid to the rights of not only the Manchu, but also of the Chinese, Mongols, and Tibetans. The Qing created their own bureaucracy but ensured that for every Manchu official appointed there was another one from one of the other groups. They were, however, determined to stamp their authority over their new domain, come what may, and they were

equally willing to use harsh measures if necessary. Authors of anti-Manchu tracts were often punished in exceptionally cruel ways; yet the Qing were also great sponsors of the arts and scholarship.

The first rulers of the Qing Dynasty adopted a friendly attitude toward those foreigners who wished to establish trade and other links with China. However, that all began to change in the eighteenth century. One emperor, Qianlong, introduced strict new laws controlling maritime trade and this commerce was limited to just one port, Guangzhou, in 1757. The trade from Guangzhou was originally in China's favor, with more exports than imports. Then, this began to change, when some European countries–Chiefly Britain–expanded their trade into opium. Although highly addictive, opium had long been popular in China, so much so that it was necessary to have it outlawed in the early eighteenth century. Nevertheless, first the Portuguese and then the British began exporting opium form elsewhere in the East and into China and in increasingly larger amounts. The Chinese authorities reacted by enacting stronger and stronger laws were to curb the trade, which had swung the balance of imports and exports strongly in favor of the westerners by the early nineteenth century, but they had little impact.

A crisis was reached in 1839, when further attempts to restrict the trade led to war with Britain, by far the largest importer. China was defeated and in 1842 was forced to sign the Treaty of Nanking (Nanjing). This left Hong Kong in British hands and opened up various other ports to foreign trade. If this was not enough turmoil, China was soon rent by a vicious uprising that began in 1850 and was destined to last for more than a decade. It was led by a mystic, Hong Xiuquin, who believed himself to be the brother of Jesus Christ. His followers were known as Tiapings and wanted to ban alcohol, opium and tobacco, but also advocated various radical social reforms. It was perhaps not surprising that they were opposed by both the Qing and various Western trading interests. The Taiping Rebellion finally ended in 1864 but cost many millions of lives and left China further weakened

Even as the rebellion was drawing to a conclusion, China became embroiled in the Second Opium War that drew in not only British, but also French and US forces. The conflict began in 1856 and China finally sued for peace four years later. The Treaty of Peking (Beijing) was as equally humiliating as its predecessor and acted as a spur for more foreign interventions on Chinese soil. There was an undeclared war with France in 1883–85; and then the Sino-Japanese War (1894–95), in which the latter country wholly humiliated China's armed forces and sparked a grab for further concessions. By the end of the century Britain, France, Russia, and Germany had control of lucrative treaty ports.

RIGHT: Bamboo is second only to rice as China's best-known crop and is a widely used material. Here, bamboo canes dry in the sun after cutting.

The exploitation of the Chinese economy by foreigners and the work of Christian missionaries within the country was greatly resented by the wider population and led to a widespread anti-foreigner movement, the Society of the Righteous Harmonious Fists, or Boxers. Resentment turned to violence and the Boxers–backed by imperial troops—laid siege to the various foreign legations in Beijing during 1900. The diplomats held out and were eventually relieved by a multinational force that, somewhat ironically, consisted of troops for virtually all of the nations that would be at each other's throats during World War I. The treaty that ended the rebellion required China to pay a huge financial penalty that further crippled an already impoverished country.

The Qing Dynasty did not survive for long after the Boxer Rebellion had ended. The dowager empress died in 1908 and a new emperor, the two-year-old Puyi, ascended the throne. The state's authority was already weak and it was ill equipped to survive the next crisis. It grew out of the large-scale foreign investment in the country's rail system that led to the creation of the Railroad Protection Movement, which began to take on an aggressively anti-Qing flavor. The city of Wuhan was seized by radical republicans and they used the movement to provoke similar uprising across China. Some two months after the unrest delegates from 17 provinces throughout the country gathered at Nanjing and the Provisional Republican Government was formed.

The government itself was established on 10 October 1911 and Sun Yatsen was named as its first president. Sun lacked the morale authority to force the dissolution of the Qing Dynasty so he turned to the ex-head of the imperial armed forces, Yuan Shikai, for help. Yuan drove a hard bargain and demanded that he be made president if he was able to negotiate the abdication of the emperor. He did as the republicans wished but Sun had to stand down in his favor. Yuan immediately dissolved the Provisional Republican Government and then changed the new constitution to make himself president for life. Many objected to this blatantly undemocratic act but Yuan went further, naming himself emperor in 1915.

Yuan's decision cost the country dear. Yunnan was the first province to secede from the new "empire". Guangxi and Guizhou followed and most of southern China came after. Troops were dispatched to the breakaway provinces but in the midst of all this turmoil Yuan died. Central authority crumbled during 1916–17 and the country dissolved into a serious of semi-autonomous regions, ruled over by competing warlords. Matters began to improve somewhat in 1919 when the victorious Allies of World War I returned the former German concession on the Shandong Peninsula to China. This sparked a wave of nationalist fervor that allowed the Kuomintang (KMT or Nationalist Party) to emerge as the dominant political force in eastern China.

The KMT was soon opposed by the Chinese Communist Party (CCP), which was established in 1921; but both were united in an uneasy alliance of sorts when it became clear that the Japanese were looking to expand into northeast China from Korea. It was only Su'sn will that prevented pro- and anti-CCP factions from tearing the KMT apart; but he died in 1925. The new leader, Chiang Kaishek, wanted to turn China into a capitalist state headed by

LEFT: This dragon, carved on a marble monument in Hohhot is a symbol that the old Chinese imperial power reached even as far a region like Inner Mongolia.

RIGHT: Traditional water filled rice terraces in the mountains of Yuanyang in Yunn.

a military dictatorship, and he wanted to undermine the CCP by expanding the KMT's authority by crushing the warlords. His so-called Northern Expedition had reached Beijing by mid-1929 and Chiang proclaimed the establishment of a national government with himself as its political and military leader.

Yet Chiang's rule did not extend to the whole of the country and even those parts that were controlled by the KMT were beset by many deep-seated social and economic problems. The CCP launched a campaign that pinpointed the KMT as the cause of these many difficulties while portraying itself as the solution. Chiang increasingly feared the spread of CCP influence, especially when an energetic new leader, Mao Zhedong, emerged. The communists had launched urban insurrections, particularly in Nanchang and Changsha, but these had been ruthlessly repressed. Mao favored a rural-based uprising but was hampered by a serious of brutal campaigns of suppression by Chiang. These did not crush the CCP entirely but made a rural-based revolt difficult to engineer. The crunch came in October 1933. Chiang launched his fifth campaign against the communists, who stood their ground despite Mao's advice to the contrary and thus suffered heavy losses. By late 1934, they had been pushed back into a small area of Jiangxi and were facing imminent annihilation.

Mao now reasserted his authority and organized a series of withdrawal northward into Shaanxi; one such became the renowned as the 5000-mile (8000-km) "Great March". It lasted a year or so and those involved experienced so many privations that only 20,000 of the original 90,000 made it to comparative safety. Nevertheless, the march made Mao the undisputed head of the CCP and many of the others that accompanied, individuals like Zhou Enlai and Deng Xiaoping, became leading figures in Chinese politics.

China's obvious lack of unity in the 1920s and beyond did not go unnoticed by the Japanese and in 1931–1932 they had taken over Manchuria. A puppet state, Manchukuo was created but the Japanese held the real power. Chiang was wholly focused on his fifth campaign against the communists and did nothing, a policy that led to both him and the KMT being roundly criticized. Much worse was to come. Japan invaded the rest of China in the middle of 1937 after engineering a spurious international incident and conducted a deliberately vicious campaign that culminated in the massacre of scores of thousands of civilians in Nanjing during December. Chiang could do little to oppose the invaders and fled, making remote Chongqing his new capital. The CCP remained behind in the Japanese-occupied areas. While it could do little to totally defeat the invaders, the CCP carried out a number of highly successful guerrilla-type operations in 1940 and also set about creating a power base from which it could challenge the KMT, once the war was over.

After Japan's surrender in 1945, the USA tried to broker a peace between the Nationalists and Communists, but civil war broke out the following year. The first major battle zone was in Manchuria and in three great battles fought during 1948–49, the Nationalist forces were soundly defeated. In fact, many Nationalists soldiers simply defected and these events led the USA

OVER PAGE: Dusk falls on Hong Kong as viewed from Victoria Peak.

to drop its support for Chiang. The writing was on the wall for the Nationalists, as the Communist momentum was by now clearly unstoppable. The latter captured Chongqing in late November 1949 and Chiang, his government, and what remained of his followers fled to the island of Formosa (Taiwan) but by then the People's Republic of China (PRC) was already in existence.

Mao Zhedong had actually announced the creation of the PRC in Beijing on 1 October 1949, but the country that the CCP had won was in a parlous state after years of conflict and neglect. The civil war had been highly destructive, the Kuomintang had been corrupt and largely left an economy in ruins and, as a parting shot, had spirited away all of its gold reserves. Agricultural output was falling away to an alarming extent and industrial production was some 50% below its pre-war levels. China also lacked much on the way of modern infrastructure – most of its 12,500 miles (20,000 km) of railroads and 30,000 miles (75,000 km) of modern roads were in need of urgent repair.

Thus the new government faced many formidable tasks yet in the first flush of victory and with much public good will, the Communists made great strides forward. The country was also unit in the face of external threats, particularly during the period of the Korean War (1950–53) when there were genuine fears that the USA might invade Chinese territory. A wide range of reforms was enacted during the decade and these involved key areas relating to both industry and agriculture as well as the monetary system. There were substantial efforts to re-energize the moribund economy during the early 1950s and these were largely successful. Inflation was brought under control, land held by large landlords was redistributed among the peasants, and industrial output was raised to prewar levels. A five-year plan was also announced and this boosted output even further.

Today, China is undergoing a phenomenal economic boom that will make it the world's largest economy in the not too distant future. It cities are expanding as rural workers flood into them in search of better wages in the new, fast-growing industries; and the country is developing a new middle class with aspirations to a western standard of living. China has joined the World Trade Organization and seems to becoming more aware of environmental issues. China's emergence into the modern, wider world is perhaps best symbolized by its hosting of the 2008 Olympics.

LEFT: Another fine, traditional gate is the South Gate entrance to Yunnan's second city of Dali.

OVER PAGE: A stone forest of eroded limestone pinnacles in Yunnan Province.

RIGHT: Children in their school uniforms parading in Beijing's Tiananmen Square.

NORTHEAST CHINA

NORTHEAST CHINA

The four provinces of Northeast China, together with the autonomous region Inner Mongolia cover an area of some 833,955 sq miles (2.175 million sq km) and the whole region, including the municipalities, has a population of some 224.8 million. As might be expected, Inner Mongolia is by far the largest, with an area of 1.183 million sq km, more than half the total, but it also has the smallest population, "just" 24.4 million people. Hebei is the most populous of the provinces (67.4 million) and Heilongjiang is the largest in area at 181,034 sq miles (469,000 sq km). Beijing at 6,485 sq miles (16,800 sq km) and Tianjin 4,386 sq miles (11,632 sq km) are home to 13.8 and 9.6 million people respectively.

Aside from the mighty Beijing and Tianjin, the various other provincial capitals vary in size considerably. Shijiazhuang, a city that really only took off with the arrival of the railroad in the first part of the twentieth century, is the capital of Hebei and has a comparatively small population of 684,000, while Heilongjiang's capital, Haerbin (Harbin), is home to 3.1 million people. Of the other two provinces, Jilin's capital, Changchun, has a population of around 2.34 million, while Liaoning's capital, Shenyang, is home to 3.5 million souls. Hohhot in Inner Mongolia boasts a more modest 1.4 million

The economic fortunes of northeast China's provinces, municipalities, and the sole autonomous region have been—and are—mixed. Coastal Hunei falls somewhat in the shadow of both Beijing and Tianjin, both of which it largely surrounds, but its economy has for long dominated by agricultural goods, mainly cotton and wheat. Heilongjiang is the country's northernmost province and has a long border with Russia that follows the course of the Amur or Heilong Jiang (Black Dragon River) that gives the province its name. Russia had a considerable impact on the province in the past, as the building of Harbin as the province's industrial heartland can attest. Nevertheless, the industrial ugliness is offset in winter by the spectacular ice sculptures that are crated there and which are wondrously illuminated at night.

Jilin, like Heilongjiang, was once part of Manchuria, and Japanese occupiers in the twentieth century kick started a process of industrialization to exploit the region's natural resources, especially around Changchun and Jilin. Changchun became home to the country's first car manufacturing plant in the 1950s.

Long and thin, Inner Mongolia runs across much of north and northeast China In stark contrast to its neighbors, it is an area of virtually unremitting grasslands fringed by the Gobi Desert in the west and bordered by

LEFT: A Tunguz tribal horse encampment bedside the Amur River. It is a scene that has changed little over the centuries.

the River Argun in the west. Life here was traditionally based around nomadic pastoralism, with sheep and horses being the main livestock. Whilst this way of life is still practiced by some of the local people, they are generally becoming more sedentary, partly through government pressure. There has also been a huge influx of Han Chinese over the last few decades and, today, Mongols make up just 15% of the total population. Industrialization has come to Inner Mongolia, particularly in the south in cities such as Hohhot and Baotou.

On the coast, Liaolong is comparatively flat in the north but there are mountains to the south. industry is now concentration around Shenyang; but Dalian (the former Port Arthur) on the Liaodong Peninsula is fast winning a reputation as the "Hong Kong of the North" as well as being a popular tourist attraction

The Northeast is, however, dominated by Beijing and Tianjin. Beijing, which actually lies outside the traditional Chinese heartland, only emerged as a cultural and political center after the Mongol invasions of the thirteenth century. Unlike many great Chinese cities it does not lie on either the coast or a major navigable river, but its significance arose because it is on the great North China Plain, a not infrequently used invasion route that needed protecting.

Beijing is both the regions and the country's unchallenged political and administrative center but Tianjin was founded on trade and greatly benefited from its relatively close proximity to the capital. This link became even more significant with the building of Grand Canal. Grain was shipped down the Yangtze to where it meets the sea, from where cargo boats sailed along the coast to Tianjin and then up the Grand Canal to Beijing. The canal was subsequently extended southward to the Yangtze, thereby removing the many dangers of sailing around the coast.

Tianjin's municipality's history in someway mirrors that of Shanghai and so the city is sometimes referred to as the "Shanghai of the North". Lying on the banks of the Hai He (Sea River), a little inland from Bohai Bay, it originally began as the trans-shipment and storage point for grain (most destined for Beijing) but it really took off when foreign traders won concessions from the Chinese authorities in the nineteenth century. However, its role as the major port in the northeast was threatened when the Hai He began to silt up, so a new port was built some 80 km downstream and thus much nearer near the open sea.

The geography of other parts of the northeast varies enormously. Hunei can be roughly divided into two zones. There are mountains and plateaux in the north, especially the Qilaotu Mountains in the northeast, while the south largely consists of mostly featureless plains flatlands.

Remote Heilongjiang is known for its bleakness in winter and has many mountainous areas, particularly in the southeast, and some of them are volcanic.

Much of the southeast of neighboring Jilin is similarly covered in mountains with dense forests and it has become something of a skiing centre

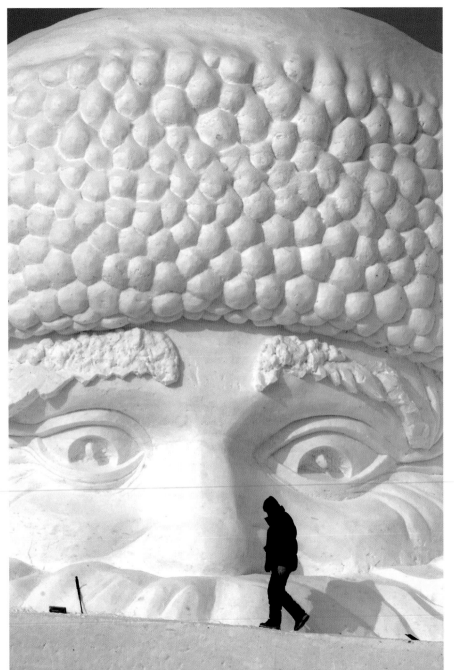

LEFT: This far northern part of China is one of the few remaining habitats of the Amur leopard (*Panthera pardus orientalis*), which is native only to the Amur River Valley, eastern Siberia, Manchuria and northern Korea.

RIGHT: Changbal Shan in Jilin is China's largest nature reserve, covering some 811 sq miles (210,000 hectares) of dense, virgin forest. Looking down through the splendor of its fall foliage, lying far below is the Yalu River. The river forms the natural and international border between China and North Korea and the name comes from a Manchu word meaning "the boundary between two fields". The Korean name of the Amnok River is simply the Korean pronunciation of the same Chinese characters.

OVERPAGE: The frontier Yalujiang Bridge, spanning the river Yalujiang-the Yalu River-from Dandong in China to North Korea on the far bank.

ABOVE: The coast near Dalian, almost at the southern-most tip of the Liaodong Peninsula, between the Yellow Sea.

RIGHT: An almost unbelievably unexpected sight is Crescent Moon Lake Oasis in the Gobi Desert, near Dunhuang along with its temple (**OVER PAGE**).

LEFT: The entrance to the Mogao Caves in the Gobi Desert. The caves, or grottoes, form a system of 492 temples and lie some 15-16 miles (25 km)(15.5 from Dunhuang. Whilst also known as the Caves of the Thousand Buddhas or the Dunhuang Caves, use of the word "cave" is rather a misnomer, as they not natural geological features. Rather, they are examples of rock-cut architecture and their murals cover 450,000 sq feet (42,000 sq m). The caves were a noted place along the old Silk Route and are probably the best known of the Buddhist grottoes-and along with the Longmen Grottoes (see pages 158 and 159) are one of the three famous ancient sculptural sites of China. In 1987, they were made a designated UNESCO World Heritage site.

RIGHT: Stupas at Mogao Caves in the Gobi Desert

LEFT: The walled city of Dunhuang stands today much as it did throughout the centuries as a major staging post on the ancient Silk Road.

RIGHT: A local girl in the colorful, traditional costume of Inner Mongolia.

40

RIGHT: The architecture of the Temple of the Five Pagodas in Hohhot (or Huhot) is very similar to that of an Indian temple. It was constructed in 1732 and within its walls there are more than 1,500 figures of Buddha.

RIGHT: A traditional herdsmen's horse race in Inner Mongolia, at the annual Nadamu Festival, Hohhot.

OVER PAGE LEFT: Mongolian yurts on Hulun Buir grassland Region in northeast China.

OVER PAGE RIGHT: This local woman is praying before an aobao, the traditional rock piles that are used as a shrine all across the wide grasslands of Inner Mongolia.

LEFT: A Buryat Mongolian man sporting a traditional pointed sheepskin cap

ABOVE: The Flaming Cliffs are in the Gobi
National Park—Gurvansaikhan —created in
1994.

OVER PAGE LEFT: The Jitong Railway, the
world's last all steam-powered railway, climbs
through the Hinggan Mountains of Inner
Mongolis.

OVER PAGE RIGHT: Elsewhere, a pair of QJ
Class 2-10-2 steam locomotives, pulling a
freight train, emerge from tunnel No, 3 on
the Jing Peng Pass section of the Jitong
Railway.

The spectacular palaces and ruins that remain from the many dynasties who have ruled China over thousands of years reveal some insight into the opulence of its past. The Beijing palace of Ming emperors was "off-limits" to most Chinese for some 500 years, hence its world-renowned name of the Forbidden City. What now remains are the largest and the best-preserved cluster of ancient buildings in China and are a designated UNESCO World Heritage site.

ABOVE: Gate of Supreme Harmony in the Forbidden City

LEFT: A corner tower on the wall and moat around part of the Forbidden City in Beijing.

OVER PAGE LEFT: Looking from Beijing's Tiananmen Square towards the Gate of Heavenly Peace entrance to the Forbidden City.

OVER PAGE RIGHT: On another side of Tiananmen Square is the Hall of Prayer for Good Harvests.

RIGHT: A contrasting, night-time scene of the Gate of Heavenly Peace, with the famous portrait of Mao Zedong strongly illuminated.

中华人民共和国万岁

OVER PAGE LEFT: Another entrance to the Forbidden City is the Supreme Harmony Gate.

OVER PAGE RIGHT: Beijing at night.

PREVIOUS PAGES: The Beijing skyline at dusk.

RIGHT: The Interior of the glass dome of the new National Grand Theater, designed by French architect Paul Andreu, during its construction in Beijing. In preparation for the 2008 Olympiad, the city saw unprecedented construction activity like nowhere else in the world.

FAR RIGHT: The section of Beijing's Second Ring Road is known as Dexengmen Xidajie.

LEFT AND RIGHT: Not far from Beijing are sections of The Great Wall, China's world-famous, awe-inspiring rampart. Although Beijing is usually the jumping-off point for tourist visits to the Great Wall, it actually stretches from Shanhaiguan on the east coast to far-flung Jiayuguan in the Gobi Desert. It was originally built in 557 CE in order to defend the Middle Kingdom from Mongol attack. Later, in the Ming Dynasty (1368 to 1644), it was substantially rebuilt. The whole of the Great wall became a s a designated UNESCO World Heritage site 1987.

OVER PAGE LEFT: The Great Wall at Badling, near Beijing.

OVER PAGE RIGHT: Snow on the steps of the Great Wall at Huangyaguan, outside of Beijing.

NORTHWEST CHINA

NORTHWEST CHINA

Northwest China consists of the country's s five most mountainous administrative areas. Three–Gansu, Qinghai and Sichuan–are classed as provinces, while Xinjiang, to the north of Tibet, is defined as an autonomous region. Taken together they have a population of some 160 million people and cover a combined area of 1.3 million sq miles (3.26 million sq km).

However, the populations and the sizes of both the provinces and administrative areas vary enormously. Sichuan, for instance, covers a relatively small area of 189, 912 sq miles (492,000 sq km), but has a population of some 88 million people. Generally, the provinces get smaller from west to east but their populations rise—but these provinces with the exception of the eastern part of Sichuan are among the most sparsely populated in the country and population densities are low outside the few large cities.

Nevertheless, for all their isolation, one of the world's truly great trading routes once passed through some of these provinces. The ancient Silk Road, which connected China with the Middle East and Europe, ran through Gansu and Xinjiang. Yet today, most of the provinces–with the notable exception of Sichuan–are relatively underdeveloped and poverty is all but endemic, especially in Gansu, Qinghai, and Xinjiang.

The Chinese government has tried to ease the isolation with large construction projects such as the Lanzhou to Urumqi railroad (completed 1963) that runs between the capitals of Gansu and Xinjiang and the recently completed controversial high-altitude rail link to Lhasa, the Tibetan capital.

However, much remains to be done and the central government's record is not very good. Qinghai, for example is used as a nuclear waste dump and is where the Chinese authorities send their "undesirables" for punishment.

This whole zone is one of China's most arid and barren and comprises a mountainous zone in the west, one that stretches from Tibet to western Sichuan from where the land is comparatively flat and much more fertile.

To the north of Tibet lies Xinjiang or the Uygher Autonomous Region. It is the largest province in the country (1.6 million sq km), making up some 16% of its total land mass and largely consists of huge desert areas to the north and south that are divided by a central mountainous spine running west to east. It capital, Urumqi, is home to 2.8 million of the autonomous region's 19.25 million inhabitants.

Gansu, which lies on Xinjiang's southeast border and is one of China's poorest provinces, is the smallest of the five but actually has the second largest population. Because much of its western area is arid and mostly uninhabitable, the greater part of its population is found in and to the east and south of its capital, Lanzhou, which has a population of some 2.8 million people. Qinghai lies to the northeast of Tibet. To the east and south of the province there are plateaux that rise up to around 3500m and there are even higher peaks on its border with Xinjiang in the northwest and along its eastern border. The province also contains the headwaters of three of Asia's mightiest rivers: the Yangtze (Chang Jiang or Chiang Jiang), the Yellow (Huang He or Hwang Ho) and Mekong. Nevertheless, much of northwest Qinghai consists of desert and salt marshes. More than 30% of the province's population, roughly 5.3 million people, is concentrated in Xining, the provincial capital and its only major city.

Sichuan means "four rivers"; but the province is actually crossed by more than 80 rivers in all, and these flow roughly west to east–from the heights

PREVIOUS PAGES: Where the Qinghai terrain permits, cultivation is extensive, as can be seen in this panoramic view of farmland.

ABOVE: A traditional-style park pavilion on the banks of the Yellow River and across from the modernized Lanzhou City.

RIGHT: THE Yellow River—Hwang-ho—passing through Eastern Qinghai.

of the northwest to the Chuanxi Plain in the east. is stark division in Sichuan's physical geography has greatly impacted upon its population density. Less than 10% of its inhabitants live in the mountainous west–which is an area dominated by the Tibetan Plateau–yet its fertile east, especially in the Sichuan basin, is home to the densest rural population in China. Sichuan is by far the most prosperous of these provinces and its booming capital, Chengdu, is the second largest in the region with a population of more than 4.1 million.

The various provinces are home to a diverse range of peoples. Tibetans previously made up the majority in their own homeland; but there is a growing Han Chinese presence; and the latter may well become the majority in the not too distant future.

The ethnic composition of Xinjiang has followed a similar pattern. Before the Communist take-over in 1949, Muslim Uyghers made up around 90% of the population. But the subsequent influx of Han had reduced the figure to below 50%. Simmering tensions between the two groups have led to not-infrequent bouts of violence and a considerable number of deaths.

Gansu is perhaps even more ethnically diverse and is home to Dongxiang, Hui, Kazakhs, Mongols, and Tibetans. Qinghai is dominated by Han Chinese but displays a similar racial mix to Gansu but with the addition of Salar and Tu minorities. Sichuan contains Han, Hui, Tibetans and Yi ethnic peoples.

With the possible exception of Sichuan, none of the provinces are currently major tourist destinations for visitors to China. Nonetheless, they have their own attractions; and with several designated UNESCO World Heritage sites, tourism is set to increase very substantially as China as a whole continues to 'open up' to the rest of the world.

Gansu, for example, has the large Labrang Monastery that is home to Buddhist monks–not only Gansu but also Inner Mongolia, Qinghai and Sichuan, while both Qinghai and Xinjiang are known for their natural beauty. Sichuan, a province that gave its name to an especially spicy cuisine, is also home to the world's largest statue of Buddha. It lies at the confluence of two rivers at Leshan and is a towering 233 feet (71m) high.

RIGHT AND FAR RIGHT: The western-most end of the Great Wall of China as it sweeps down the hills to the fortress city of Jiayuquan, with its magnificent equestrian statue.

FAR LEFT: The ancient walls and fort of Jiayuguan itself.

LEFT: Elsewhere in Gansu, this impressive sculpture of Maitreya Buddha is in the great tourist site of Bingling Si— the Bingling Grottoes.

OVER PAGE LEFT: Motorboats moored on the Liujiaxia Reservoir, on the Yellow river, near the Bingling Grottoes.

OVER PAGE RIGHT: In these mountains, rising from the Quighai-Tibet Plateau, Chinese scientists claimed in the spring of 2007 to have induced rainfall by means of cloud seeding.

FAR LEFT AND LEFT: Many tributaries, like this one of dark, silt-laden waters in Qinghai, feed the infant Yellow River.

RIGHT: A wintry scene of a village situated near Pianguan alongside the Yellow River—once also called the Hwang Ho, but now named the Huang He.

LEFT: Qinghai's Dragon Fur River Valley and its encircling mountains.

RIGHT: A satellite view of Qinghai Lake, the largest in the region and fed by several rivers, including the Buh (left).

FAR LEFT: The Qinghai-Tibet Railway connecting remote Lhasa to China, via Golmud, was completed in 2006 with some 3,123 miles (1,956 km) of track. The line is the world's highest altitude railway project, reaching altitudes of over 16,500 feet (5,000 m) above sea level. Here the railway crosses an impressive bridge and then winds its way through the Kunlun Mountain Range in the Wudaoliang area of Qinghai province (**inset**).

LEFT: Qinghai is evolving modern industries like many parts of modern China. This flower farm, although located in an altitude of 6,600 feet (2,200 m) in the freezing cold city of Xining, uses modern technology in greenhouses for commercial flower production. The flowers sell well, especially as the Chinese New Year approaches and people begin to decorate their home.

LEFT: Aerial view of a village along the Yellow Riverin Qinghai Province.

OVER PAGE LEFT: More traditional is the Red Sect Buddhist monastery at Archon, Baima.

OVER PAGE RIGHT: The Tibetan Plateau, including the area lying within Qinghai, is home to a rare species of wild ass (*Equus hemionus kiang*), whose herds still manage to survive in this harsh environment.

ABOVE: Ornate bronze temple bells hanging at the Wu Hou shrine in Chengdu, Sichuan. Dedicated to the Minister of War, it commemorates Zhuge Liang, a much-respected military strategist from the Three Kingdoms period. The site dates from 223 CE, when one of his commanders, Liu Bei, was buried here.

RIGHT: Also at Wu Hou Shrine can be seen the famous Tang Tablet (also known as the Tablet of Three Excellences) which dates from 809 CE. This detail shows the very finest examples of traditional composition, calligraphy and carving, with the work still being clearly indicated as having been executed by Dei Du, Liu Gongchuo and Lu Ten, respectively.

FAR RIGHT: Candles burn with incense in front of the Si Yan Temple, which forms another part of the Wu Hou Shrine. Lui Bei himself, Guan Yu and Zhang Fei swore brotherhood to each other—hence its alternative name of the temple of the Three Righteous Brothers

FAR LEFT: Another feature of the Wu Hou Shrine at Chengdu is this 1672 statue of the army commander Liu Bei himself, the founder of the Shu Kingdom.

LEFT: When the Wu Hou Ci site was expanded between 1662 and1672, the work included the addition of halls and statuary of Three Kingdoms' characters to guard and enhance Liu Bei's tomb. This guardian lion is just one of many examples.

RIGHT: Traditional mask-changing costumed dancers performing on the stage of the Theatre of Wu Hou Shrine. Frequent performances of Three Kingdoms rituals, Sichuan Opera, mask-changing dancers, puppet shows, shadow plays etc. Leading to the theatre is ancient Jin Li street, which Is alive with tea houses, food stalls, restaurants and silk and embroidery crafts and souvenirs.

FAR LEFT: The imposing approach and entrance to Yongling Museum, also in Chengdu and tomb of the Sichuan emperor Wang Jian, who ruled the region over the period 907-918 CE

LEFT: This stone warrior stands guard outside the tomb mound of Wang Jian at Yongling. The site is also famous for the carvings on the stone platform, which support a wooden sarcophagus inside the tomb. They show an orchestra of 22 female figures playing different traditional Chinese musical instruments.

LEFT: Chengdu is also the site of the Qingyang temple. It is often called Green Goat or Green Ram Temple because of the two Tang dynasty bronze statues of rams or goats in the Hall of the Three Purities, one of the main halls at the temple site. Here is one of the bronzes standing in front of the figure of the Heavenly Lord of the Numinous Treasure in the Highest Clarity Realm. Founded in the 9th century, Qingyang is a major centre of Taoist, pilgrimage which is related to its founder, Laozi, is said to have been recognized in re-incarnation when seen as a boy leading goats through a Chengdu market. In fact, the name Qingyang means "green goat."

RIGHT: This bronze dragon motif is part of an incense stand at the Qingyang temple site of Taost pilgrimage.

LEFT: Small boats like these in Sichuan still ply the Yangtze River. Despite modern development and Three Gorges Dam (see page 190), it remains the great waterway and means of traversing great areas of China

BELOW: The Jiuzhaigou area of Sichuan is a spectacular nature reserve scattered with high alpine peaks, hundreds of clear lakes and lush forests. It was first settled by ethnic Tibetans and their traditions are still evident in the shrines, prayer wheels and prayer flags that decorate the region-such as this giant head of the rock-cut Grand Buddha at Leshan.

ABOVE: The Grand Buddha is painted on a giant carving into the red sandstone of the Yangtze River canyon wall in Sichuan. Standing some 2340 feet (71 m) high, it is the largest depiction in the world. Work on this enormous figure lasted more than 90 years and its sheer size and the monumentality of this artistic feat are truly breathtaking.

LEFT: Tents with traditional Buddhist designs at Sichuan's Litang Horse Festival.

OVER PAGE LEFT: Sichuan's Shuiluo He River valley in the Shaluli Shan mountain range.

OVER PAGE RIGHT: The tranquility of Heaven Lake, which lies surrounded by the Tian Shan mountains of Xinjang. The lake is sacred to both the local Tibetans and Sala Muslims, and is set in a lush valley of verdant alpine forest.

LEFT: The natural beauty of the region is evident in scenes like this of the Nuorilang Waterfall

TOP RIGHT: The nature reserve is also a haven for wildlife, including the red panda (*Ailurus fulgens*), here amidst the mountain snows.

BELOW RIGHT: The red panda's related species is probably one of China's best-known mammals and is loved throughout the world. As well as being the international symbol of the WWF, the giant panda (*Ailuropoda melanoleuca*, meaning "black-and-white cat-foot") was chosen as one of the mascots for the Beijing Olympics of 2008. Sichuan is home to its major natural reserve and of China's Giant Panda Breeding Research Base at Chengdu and the Sichuan giant panda reserve became a designated UNESCO World Heritage site in 2006.

LEFT: Whilst the Taklimakan Desert is flanked by high mountain ranges, such as the Kunlun Mountains, its wind-blown sand cover also includes some strangely weathered shaped rocky outcrops. Here, an adventurous climber scales a cliff in the shadow of Shipton's Arch, a particularly spectacular example of such natural features.

ABOVE A camel caravan crossing the Taklimakan Desert near Dunhuang in Xingjian. These days, although once part of the ancient Silk Route, such caravan-type expeditions are a notable tourist attraction for the more adventurous traveler.

OVER PAGE LEFT: This ancient, traditional Chinese statue stands at a popular tourist site that is a starting point for camel train expeditions into the Taklimakan Desert. Forming the greater part of the Tarim River basin of Xinjiang, it is one of the world's largest sandy wastes, and is about 600 miles (965 km) across, with an area of 105,000 sq miles (272,000 sq km). The name Taklimakan derives from "the taking up of waters" as rivers only penetrate the desert for some 60-120 miles (100-200 km) before drying up in its wind-blown sand, which are as deep as 1,000 ft (300 m) and with pyramidal dunes that can reach 1,000 feet (300 m) in height.

OVER PAGE RIGHT: Although under Chinese sovereignty, Islamic Kashgar in Xinjiang is over 2370 miles (3,800 km) from Beijing, yet less than 250 miles (400 km) from Pakistan, Tajikistan and Afghanistan. Here, a crowd gathers in Kashgar to watch Uyghur women in traditional dress perform a folk dance.

FAR LEFT: The Abakh Hoja Tombin in Kashi is typically Islamic in its design and architectural features.

LEFT: The donkey cart remains a standard form of Uyghur tansport in Kashi, within the Autonomous Region.

ABOVE: An Islamic Uyghur woman walks beside pottery on sale in the historic old quarter of Kashgar during the ongoing Muslim holy month of Ramadan.

FAR LEFT: The ruins of the ancient city of Jiaohe lie in Xinjiang's Uyghur Autonomous Region.

LEFT: Near Turpan in Xinjiang's Uyghur Region

OVER PAGE LEFT: The south of Xinjiang is home to another religion. Here, Tibetan Buddhists and pilgrims turn prayer wheels as they walk the perimeter of the Labrang Monastery, which lies beneath Phoenix Mountain on the old Silk Road. True believers consider that only turning the wheels 10,00 times will bring about true salvation-the task of a lifetime.

OVER PAGE RIGHT: Until now, tourist like these gazing down upon the activities of the monks and pilgrims at Labrang Monastery will probably have had a long and arduous journey to their destination. But the traditional way of life of the ethnic Tibetan population and nomadic lifestyle of the area are threatened by the proposal for the building of a major airport, with a vast increase in visitors and associated effects of the outside world.

Left: Camels on the Pamir Plateau, alongside the Karakoram Highway in Kashgar.

Below: Mount Mingshan, Dunang, is a popular tourist destination, where visitors can ride camels to the home of the "King of Hell."

TIBET

TIBET

It was the Qing dynasty that first made Tibet a Chinese colony in 1751, but there was little real affect on its traditional culture and religious beliefs, It was some 200 years later when things truly began to change when the new Chinese Communist regime occupied Tibet by force in 1 949–50, taking total control by 1959 and designating it to be an autonomous region of China itself

Most of Tibet is one vast plateau that rises up to between 13,000 and 16,400 feet (4000 m and 5000 m), and gets higher from east to west. It is dissected by many large rivers that have carved out steep-sided valleys, including the Yarlung Tsangpo, the autonomous region's heartland.

To the southwest stands the famed holy peak of Mount Kailas, one of the most revered pilgrimage sites for Hindus, Buddhists, Jains and Bonpos (pre-Buddhists) and its location is virtually the source four of some of Asia's great rivers, including the Indus and.

Tibet, as now defined, by China has an area of nearly 500,000 sq miles (1.2 million sq km) but a population of just 2.7 million. Tibetans previously made up the majority of people in their own homeland but there is an ever-growing Han Chinese presence and the latter may well become the majority in the not too distant future.

The Chinese government has tried to ease the isolation with large construction projects such as the recently completed, controversial high-altitude rail link to Lhasa, the Tibetan capital. The 714-mile (1142-km) Golmud–Lhasa line links the province of Qinghai with the capital–and by extension connects the cities of Lhasa and with Beijing. The trains were specially designed to operate in the extreme conditions of the 13,200-feet (4,000-m) Tibetan Plateau, where temperatures regularly drop to minus 10^0F (-35^0C) and 50-mph (80-kph) winds act as an "ecological sandblaster". In its initial runs, the vast majority of passengers on the new line were Han Chinese migrant workers, entrepreneurs and tourists. Heavy re-branding by the Beijing government has helped turn Tibet into a popular tourist destination. In an attempt to enrich the cultural experience for Chinese tourists, many Tibetan families who live near the line have been forced into rebuilding their houses in a specific "authentic" style. Subsidies have available to help pay for the renovations, but most families are now burdened with financial debt and, ironically, are unlikely ever to be afford travel on the train.

Lhasa is renowned for its many Buddhist religious sites, the most famous of which is the UNESCO World Heritage site of the Potala Palace, the impressive former residence of Tibet's spiritual leader the Dalai Lama. Despite his flight from Tibet in 1959-60 and subsequent exile, the Potala remains one of the holiest sites in Tibetan Buddhism and dominates the Lhasa skyline.

Opposition to the Chinese suzerainty of Tibet remains an international cause, coupled with concerns about the possible environmental effect on this unique region by industrial and engineering developments.

PREVIOUS PAGES: Mount Kailas at 22,028 feet (6,714 m) is a famed holy peak to the north of the Himalayas in Western Tibet. This legendary snow-shrouded rock dome is one of the most revered pilgrimage sites for Hindus, Buddhists, Jains and Bonpos (pre-Buddhists). It draws pilgrims from allover Asia and from other parts of the world. A runs down its slopes into Manasarovar Lake, from which flow four of Asia's great rivers-the Indus, Brahmaputra, Karnali and the Sutlej.

LEFT: The Samye Monastery—Samye Compa—at Dranang was built in approximately 775 CE by order of the Tibetan King Triosong Detsen, who wanted to revitalize Buddhism, which had declined since its introduction by a previous king, Songsten Gampo a century before. (Puning Temple at Chengde in China's Hubei province was beased very much upon Samye Compa.

Left: Drogpa nomads herd Yaks above Kangshung Glacier, east of Mt. Everest; Chomolonzo Peak is seen in the distance, Tibet.

Right: A narrow stream runs down the center of a green Tibetan valley in the Amne Machin massif-a mountain group which has had some controversy as to its true height over the decades, but which is now agreed to be 20, 610 feet (6282 m) at its highest point,

PREVIOUS PAGES: Sand dunes close by Samye Monastery.

LEFT: This wall painting of Amitayus, a Tibetan Buddhist deity, can be found at Tagong Monastery.

RIGHT: On the Tibetan Buddhist festival known as Labab Duchen, pilgrims circumnavigate a hill near Nagqu, on which stands a stupa. The most devout will carry this out by repeatedly prostrating themselves as they pass around the site.

PREVIOUS PAGE LEFT: A nomadic sheep herd on the seemingly endless Tibetan plains.

PREVIOUS PAGE RIGHT: At an altitude of 15.570 feet (4718 m), the sacred lake of Nam-tso is approximately 300 miles (190 km) north of Lhasa and its surprisingly salty waters are a stunning shade of turquoise. As a place of pilgrimage, so-called *mani* stones and stupa can be found on its shores.

RIGHT: The Tibetan plateau and hills that border the sacred lake of Nam-tso.

FAR RIGHT: Gyangze Town, 13,250ft above sea level, nestles in mountains in southern Tibet.

OVER PAGE: The Nam-tso River

RIGHT AND FAR RIGHT: The Potala Palace, the dazzling former winter residence of the Dalai Lama, is one of the holiest sites in Tibetan Buddhism. It dominates the skyline of Lhasa and was once the centre of the Tibetan government. Standing 13 storeys tall, the Potala is one of the architectural wonders of the world and has been a designated UNESCO World Heritage site since 1994.

LEFT: The Potala Palace.

RIGHT: Gold Ornamentation on the summit of a temple in Lahsa.

OVER PAGE LEFT: Yamdrok-tso ("upper pasture lake") is another turquoise blue lake about 160 miles (100 km) to the southwest of Lhasa. With an area of 265 sq miles (678 sq km) and an altitude of 14,655 feet (4,441 m), it drains a huge watershed area. Although the third largest lake on the Tibetan Plateau, it has no outlet and no perennial source of water, although snow from the surrounding mountains occasionally melts to feed the lake. Sacred to Tibetan Buddhists, its status and future have become a cause celebré, as—against world-wide environmental protest—the Chinese government plans, controversially, to drop the water level through some 2,800 feet (846 m) to a hydroelectric station.

OVER PAGE RIGHT: Two climbers at sunrise on Gurla Mandnata. Called Naimona'nyi by the local Tibetans, it is the highest peak in southwestern Tibet at 25,242 feet (7694 m). It stands south of Lake Manasarowar, not far north of the point where Nepal, Tibet and India meet and was only first climbed as recently as 1985.

CENTRAL CHINA

CENTRAL CHINA

Central China consists of six provinces and one autonomous region, and all are landlocked apart from two; Jiangsu and Shandong. The other provinces lying in the interior are Anhui, Henan, Ningxia—an autonomous region— Shaanxi, and Shanxi. They cover of area of 38,210 sq miles (989,900 sq km) in total. The largest in terms of area is Shaanxi at 79,130 sq miles (205,000 sq km), while the smallest is Ningxia at a comparatively small 25,630 sq miles (66,400 sq km).

Central China has a combined population of some 406 million. The most populous provinces is Henan with 95.5 million people but this figure is almost matched by Shandong's 93.4 million. The smallest, once again, is Ningxia on the northern edge of the central zone with just 5.9 million. The other provinces range between 30-40 million (Shaanxi and Shanxi) and 60-80 million (Anhui and Jiangsu). Shanxi, which is largely mountainous, has the second smallest population at 33.8 million but is actually the third biggest province

The provinces' capital cities show a similar range of populations. Hefei in central Anhui has a population of 4.2 million, Zhengzhou, the hub of rail communications in Henan, has 6.2 million, while Nanjing, one of the country's most booming cities, lies in Jiangsu and is home to 5.3 million. Underpopluated Ningxia's capital is Yinchuan and it has a populace of just one million, while Xian in the much larger Shaanxi to the southeast has some 6.6 million. The capital of coastal Shandong, Jinan, is home to 1.96 million but this is almost matched by Qingdao, a major commercial hub, with 1.6 million. Shanxi's capital, Taiyuan, lies in the virtual center of the province and has a population of around 2.9 million.

Anhui is one of China's least modernized provinces in part due to its harsh geography, which makes traditional agriculture a marginal activity at best. There have been attempts to improve the local transport infrastructure in the recent past but much remains to be done.

Henan to the northwest of Anhui is considered one of the cradles of Chinese history but even today its economy remains dominated by agriculture. Jiangsu's comparative wealth was built on the province having some of China's most productive land and it also became a major centre of the communications as the Yangtze flows through the south before entering the Yellow Sea. It is one of China's fastest-growing provinces with heavy industry mostly found around Nanjing, while the smaller cities and towns are dominated by light manufacturing.

Ningxia was only created as an autonomous region in 1958 and has a mostly underdeveloped economy. There is farming around the Huang He and

the irrigation systems that run off it but the desert south of the region is far to arid to be worked. Many locals migrate to industrial cities in neighboring provinces like Hohhot in Inner Mongolia to the north and Lanzhou in Gansu to the south.

Unlike isolated Ningxia, with which it shares a short border, Shaanxi, has long played a central part in Chinese history and it economy was originally dominated by marginal farming but trade with distant lands was also important as the Silk Road terminated there. Today, it is renowned as a major tourist attraction; but the province is also rich in both coal and oil.

Shandong on the east coast is one of the country's most prosperous provinces and has a long-established history of international trade. Major European powers established concession along its coast during the nineteenth century, including the British at Weihei and the Germans at Qingdao. Jinan, its capital, is something of a minor boom town, but the coastal cities, especially Qingdao, still dominate the bustling and expanding local economy. Northeast

PREVIOUS PAGES: The Yellow Mountains, the Huang Shan, in Anhui.

ABOVE: In Nanjing, ancient capital of the South, the buildings which make up the Mausoleum of Sun Yatsen—founder of the People's Republic of China in 1911—were begun a year after his death in 1925. The finished version, a traditionally Ming-style tomb, has become a place of pilgrimage for people wishing to pay their respects to the father of modern China. Visitors have to climb the impressive stone steps leading up to the mausoleum itself.

RIGHT: Replicas of banner men of the Ming dynasty guard the old Zhonghua Gate of southern Nanjing.

Shandong also contains Shengli, China's second biggest oilfield. Power is also at the heart of the economy of relatively impoverished Shanxi and something like 33% of the country's coal (and iron ore) is extracted from the province. This has come at an enormous environmental price as northern Shanxi contains many of the most polluted towns and cities in China, such as Datong and Taiyuan.

Anhui can be split into two distinct but equally inhospitable zones – the north is dominated by arid flatlands that are part of the North China Plain, while the south is mainly mountainous. The mighty Yangtze flows through the lower part of this area and is liable to flood in both spring and summer. The Yellow River, or Huang He, flows across the northern portion of Henan and its importance is reflected in the province's name, which means "South of the River".

Henan lacks much mountainous terrain except perhaps in the south and something like 60% of its land area is classified as plain. Jiangsu's south is dominated by the delta of the Yangtze and the north is an area a fertile land of lakes and irrigation canals.

The Yellow Rover flows along the northern border of Ningxia but the autonomous region is largely an area of arid mountains. Another river, the Wei He, flows west-to-east through central Shaanxi and to its south lie the Qinling Mountains, while to the north lie arid plateaux.

In contrast to the previous two provinces, Shandong is effectively a peninsula surrounded by water on three sides but also contains the lower reaches of the Yellow River.

Shanxi lies to the east of its similarly named neighbor Shaanxi and its name actually means "West of the Mountains". This refers to the fairly modest range known as Taihang Shan that lie along Shanxi's eastern border–but, in fact, something like 70% of the province is classified as being mountainous. The province's deep sense of isolation is compounded by the Yellow River, which flows down its western and eastern borders. The Gobi Desert lies to the north of the province in Inner Mongolia

In terms of population, Central China is largely dominated by ethnic Chinese, but these are some minorities to be found there. Anhui, for example, has a minority of Muslim Hui people, although Ningxia was actually created as a homeland for them. Yet, there has been a major diaspora of the people over time and only 20% of the Hui actually now live in Ningxia. Most have moved in search of employment, as Ningxia is one of China's poorest provinces.

LEFT: A classic line of cargo boats near Nanjing, on the Grand Canal, the longest artificial waterway in the world.

ABOVE: Suzhou's Taihu Lake is also the location of the classical Chinese gardens that were designated a UNESCO World heritage site in 1997.

RIGHT: A veritable traffic jam of river barges on the Grand Canal at Suzhou, north of Nanjing.

OVER PAGE LEFT: Chinese children at a kindergarten school in the farm village town of Buyang near the northern city of Jinan city in Shandong.

OVER PAGE RIGHT: A market day scene in northern China, in the farming village of Hul Wen, Shandong. A communal motor scooter carries goods and produce, as well has the elderly and disabled.

CHINA | CENTRAL CHINA

LEFT: A giant statue standing on Thousand Buddha Mountain—or Qianfo Shan—on the edge of Jinan city, Shandong. Construction of the Thousand Buddha Temple started in the Sui Dynasty (581 to 618 CE), but its name was changed to Xingguo Monastery in the Tang Dynasty The building was again extended In the Ming Dynast and became a well-known place of pilgrimage. Many other statues and rock carvings adorn the surrounding hillsides, hence Qianfo Shan's more popular name of Thousand Buddha Mountain.

RIGHT: Xingguo Monastery now contains within it the Main Temple, the Bodhisattva House, Maitreya Temple and the Duihua Pavilion-all enriched by wonderful temple effigies such as that pictured here.

FAR RIGHT: Buddhist monks inside Xingguo Monastery.

PREVIOUS PAGE LEFT: The monastery's roof tiles are an artistic treasure in themselves, with their butterfly and dragon-head motifs.

PREVIOUS PAGE RIGHT: A more modern development within the same region is this hydroelectric project on the Yellow River about 25 miles (40 km) south of the city of Jinan. Here, the feeder reservoir dam can be seen under construction.

LEFT: Typical of the work carried out in the craft workshops near Jinan Zbo is this magnificent dragon carving on a traditional Longshan black pottery vase.

RIGHT: Traditional dim sum, Chinese dumplings in farm kitchen in Shandong.

RIGHT: Tai Shan is the most revered of the five sacred Taoist mountains of China, this mountain in Shandong is shrouded in mystique and legend. Imperial sacrifices were offered from its summit; and even today, upon climbing its heights, it is easy understand why the site was chosen. It became a UNESCO Wolrd heritage site in 1987.

RIGHT: Pilgrims on the Stairway to Heaven leading to the Gateway to Heaven Temple at the summit of Mount Tai Sha

FAR LEFT: Tai Shan is also called Eastern Mountain. As an important place of pilgrimage, its slopes and valleys are the sites of many sacred temples, paths and shrines-like this pavilion high on the mountain's eastern flanks.

LEFT: On Tai Shan, the God of Eastern Mountain himself is depicted in the temple yard of South Heavenly Gate-or Nan Tian Men-which guards the final approach for pilgrims on their way to the summit of the sacred peak.

RIGHT: Traditionally, pilgrim couples seeking good fortune and a happy future attach padlocks to the Incense stand in the temple yard of the South Heavenly Gate.

OVER PAGE LEFT: The monastery gate and courtyard of the Palace (or temple) of the Heavenly Queen, also known as Fujian Guildhall, in the Shandong port of Yantai. It is dedicated to Maze (or Lin Mo), who is traditionally associated with the protection and blessing of vessels on the sea and temples to her are found along the long Chinese coastline. Construction of this example, which was financed by shipping traders and merchants from Fujian Province, started in 1884.

OVER PAGE RIGHT: The Temple of the Heavenly Queen is also known as the Yantai Museum and is famous for its very fine wood and stone carvings, and for architectural details in its painted roof beams, like these in the museum complex which depict scenes from Chinese history and folk legends.

LEFT: The port of Yantai's ice-free harbour and dock facility as seen at sunset from the Yantai Hill lighthouse.

FAR LEFT: Finely carved marble dragon-coiled columns at the Confucius Temple in Qufu.

FAR LEFT: As well as being Shandong's major metropolis, Yanati is a thriving seaport, as is evident in the new Port Authority Custom, Building, which rises up in the city centre.

LEFT: The splendid Seven-Story Pagoda in Anhui. The nearby ancient villages of Xidi and Hongcun became UNESCO World Heritage sites in 2000.

ABOVE: The Huang Shan—the Yellow Mountains—in Anhui are probably China's most famous mountain attraction. With gnarled pines, craggy rocks and a rolling sea of clouds, it is if nothing else almost the epitome and most evocative image that is associated evocative of a Chinese ink painting.

OVER PAGE LEFT: The Longmen Grottoes and their magnificent carved statues above the Yi River in Hennan have been another of the UNESCO designated World Heritage sites in China since 2000.

OVER PAGE RIGHT: A magnificent statue of Buddha in the Fengxian Cave of the Longmen Grottoes

RIGHT: Looking southeast, over the sharp ridges of the Qingling Mountains southwest of Xian, which separate the provinces of Shaanxi and Sichuan.

OVER PAGE LEFT: Hukou ('Pot Spout'), a waterfall on the Yellow River, is a spectacular natural feature that separates Shanxi and Shaanxi provinces.

OVER PAGE RIGHT: Almost sculptural in their creation are these terraced fields near Sanmenxia along the Yellow River.

LEFT AND RIGHT: The Army of Terracotta Warriors were a major world archeological discovery when the underground vaults were first explored in Shaanxi in 1974. Excavations eventually revealed more than 8,000, life-size soldiers and their horses, all modeled from terracotta. Arranged in battle formation, they represent the armed retinue of unified China's first emperor, Qin Shi Huang Ti. The figures are over 2,000 years old and are amazingly well preserved. Consequently, they are now a major archaeological and tourist attraction of universal renown.

FAR RIGHT: The striking face of one of the Terracotta Warriors.

PREVIOUS PAGE LEFT: Ancient stone carving of a galloping horse at the Maoling Mausoleum near Xian, Shaanxi. It is just one of a group of 16 famous 2000-year-old, life-size stone depictions from the Western Han Dynasty (206 BCE to 24 CE) that were carved with iron and steel tools out of the pegmatite stone, which is as hard as marble. They stand outside of the tomb of the heroic general Huo Qubing, who gained several important victories over the northern Hun. Upon his early death, Emperor Wu Di ordered the general's tomb to be constructed beside his own in the Maoling Mausoleum complex, some 80 km northwest of Xian. The group of carvings are highly regarded internationally as being exceptional examples of early Chinese art.

PREVIOUS PAGE RIGHT: One of the pair of 1200-year-old stone lions that guarded the four inner walls of the Qianling Mausoleum. It stands in front of the Tang Dynasty tomb of emperor Gao Zong (also called Li Zhi) and empress Wu Zetian (also called Wu Zhao). Li Zhi ruled from 649 to 683 CE and Wu Zetain from 684 to 705. In the far distance is the tree-covered Liangshan Mountain where lies the actual burial mound for the tomb.

CENTRE: 1200 years old and known as Shi Ong Zhong or Weng Zhong. They line the spirit path leading to the tomb of Tang Dynasty emperor Li Zhi and empress Wu Zetian.

RIGHT AND FAR RIGHT: Also at the Qianling Mausoleum stand a range of carved stone guardian soldiers and horse.

LEFT: Dawn breaking on the old city walls of Ping Yao in Shanxi. With a history of more than 1600 years, the medieval city was placed on the UNESCO World Heritage List in 1997.

RIGHT AND BELOW: Rooftops and walkway and roofs of a Buddhist temple in Ping Yao.

One of the most holy peaks of Chinese
Buddhism, Mount Wutai (or Wutaishan) lies
in Wutai in the Xinzhou region of Shanxi
and is rated amongst the highest of all
China's national scenic spots. The whole
Wutaishan mountain area covers an area of
1,095 sq miles (2,837 sq km) and its five
main peaks, positioned east, south, west,
north, and in the middle, embrace one
another with broad and plain terraces rather
than forests on their tops. That is why it
bears the name Wutaishan ("Mountain of
Five Terraces"). With the average altitude
over 3,281 feet (1,000 m), its apex is the
summit of the northern peak and is famed
as being the "Roof of Northern China",
reaching 10,043 feet (3,061 m). Besides its
religious significance, the beauty of its rising
and falling mountain ridges, criss-crossed
gullies, crystalline waters and towering green
forests also add to Wutaishan's reputation as
a spectacular and noted tourist destination.

RIGHT: Pilgrims and tourists walk near the
Pusading Monastery in the Wutai Mountains
of China.

CENTRE: This amazing statue of Buddha
emerging from a mechanical giant lotus
flower stands in the monastery pagoda at
Wutai.

FAR RIGHT: The Big White Pagoda at
Taihuai in the Wutaishan Mountains,
Xinzhou region of Shanxi.

OVER PAGE LEFT: A detail of the Nine
Dragons Wall at Datong.

OVER PAGE RIGHT: Monks kneel down at
prayer during a Buddhist ceremony held on
the sacred Wutai Mountain.

SOUTHEAST CHINA

SOUTHEAST CHINA

PREVIOUS PAGES: A panorama of Shanghai's modern skyline, with a view of Pudong (to the left) and of the Huangpu River.

RIGHT: The Huangpu River rolls past many of the new towers of Pudong, including the Oriental Pearl TV Tower, the tallest, and the pagoda shaped Jin Mao Building.

Southeast China comprises five provinces and the bustling municipality of Shanghai, Chinese biggest city and a fast-expanding economic powerhouse. The provinces of Fujian, Hubai, Hunan, Jiangxi and Zhejiang together cover some 344,300 sq miles (892,000 sq km) and have a combined population of around 270 million. Fujian is the most extensive of the provinces at about 87,622 sq miles (227,000 sq km), while Zhejiang is the smallest at some 39,370 sq miles (102,000 sq km). The provinces' populations vary considerably. Hunan is the largest with more than 70 million inhabitants while the smallest Jiangxi has some 43 million. Rapidly expanding Shanghai is home to 13.2 million Chinese citizens.

While Shanghai is the largest city in the region by some margin and is unlikely to lose its status, many of the southeast's provincial capitals are of a significant—and growing—size. The bustling port of Fuzhou in Fijian has 5.8 million inhabitants and Nanchang in Jiangxi has more than 4 million In addition, Changsa in Hunan has more than 5.8 million, Wuhan in Hubei over 8.3 million, and Hangzhou in Zhejiang boasts close to 6.2 million people. Continuing rural-to-urban migration by the poor will almost certainly ensure that all will grow apace over the following decades.

This wave of migration is a good indicator that many of the provinces are undergoing rapid economic development, especially those along the coast or the one in the interior that have major rivers flowing though them. Fujian has a number of ports and some, like Fuzhou and Xiamen, remain important trading or financial centers attracting overseas investment, while others that where once important, such as Quanzhou, have lost some of their old dominance but retained their charm.

Hubei's economy has long been dominated by agriculture because of its fertility of the province's soil but it also contains Wuhan, a major river port that is expanding quickly as trade along the Yangtze River continues to boom.

Hunan is the fifth most productive province in China, with a local economy dominated by agriculture and much of that trade flowed through its capital Changsa, which grew up along the banks of the Xian River (Xiang/Xian Jiang).

Jiangxi is by no means one of the southeast's great economic powerhouses, despite having a long-established porcelain industry and its capital, Nanchang, has less of the hustle and bustle of its coastal equivalents. Zhejiang is yet another coastal province and, despite being one of the country's smallest, it is also one of its most prosperous. Its economy was based on it being able to produce agricultural surpluses to feed other parts of China, but Hangzhou also became a major international trading port.

It is Shanghai, however, that is economically and culturally pre-eminent in the southeast. It name means "by the sea" and this title gives some indication of how its early prosperity was won. Originally a small fishing village, it underwent a rapid transformation after it was granted to the British as a concession port in 1842 and other many other foreign nations followed to create what became known as the International Settlement. Opium, tea, and silk were the first trade goods but these export-import businesses were followed by the investment houses that had made the city the financial hub of the Far East by the late nineteenth century. Shanghai declined somewhat after the Communist takeover in 1949, as the country became something of a closed economy. Then, it was re-energized in the 1990s, after China's central government decided to allow its own form of free enterprise to return to the city.

LEFT: High-rise office towers and skyscrapers of Pudong Economic Zone at night.

The geography of the five provinces varies considerable. Fujian has a largely mountainous interior but some ranges are also found along the coast, while land-locked Hubei on the region's northern edge can be divided in three zones. Roughly two-thirds of the province consists of gently undulating land drained by the Chiang Kiang and Han rivers that gives way to increasingly high ground dissected by river valleys that forms the border with Sichuan.

Finally, the final zone is mountainous and heavily forested. In all something like 70% of Hubei is classified as hilly or mountainous and it is famed for its many lakes. The basin of the Yangtze, which flows into the province in the northeast along its border with Hubei, dominates Hunan's central area but to the east, south and west are increasingly mountainous areas.

Jiangxi, sandwiched between Fujian and Hunan, is dominated by trees; something over 60% of the province is classified by forest with much of it in mountainous areas. Yet the province lies on the middle and lower reaches of the mighty Yangtze. This river—along with many others– is a major source water for much of Southeast China. Maritime Zhejiang can be readily divided into two main areas. North of the capital, Hangzhou, lies a flat plain, much of which is part of the Yangtze's large delta, while the area to the south is much more mountainous and is an extension of the upland region of neighboring Fujian to the south.

The municipality of Shanghai stretches over a large area; but the heart of the city is effectively divided by the Huangpu River. West of the Huangpu, lies the area known as Puxu in which many of the city's older tourist attractions are found including the Bund, once the financial heart of the city. Pudong lies to the east of river and up until the early 1990s it was a partly boggy area known for nothing more than vegetable farming but today it has replaced the Bund as Shanghai's financial center. It skyscrapers now stand in stark contrast to the comparatively low-rise tower blocks of the Bund

The southeast is also home to a variety of peoples, many of who tend to congregate in various mountainous areas, but Han Chinese remain the leading group. Hubei in the interior is, like its neighbors, dominated by Han China but also contains significant pockets of other minorities including Hui, Miao, Mongol and Tujia. Hunan, also landlocked, is home to an equally diverse range of people. Once again Han are predominant, but a number of minorities found in its mountain areas include the Dong, Miao, Tujia, and Uyghers.

RIGHT: A mass tai chi exercise taking place along the Bund.

LEFT: Bright, modern neon signs light up Nanjing Lu, Shanghai's main shopping street.

RIGHT: Shanghai Grand Theatre, People's Square, Shanghai.

OVER PAGE: The Bund, Huangpu River and Pudong night skyline of Shanghai. The Bund itself is probably China's most famous street. It faces Huangpuliang and features an assortment of buildings in European neoclassical 1930s styles. Almost ironically, its architecture provides a nostalgic echo of a bygone, colonialist and imperialistic era.

LEFT: The old town of Wushan along the Yangtze River will almost certainly be submerged after the completion of the Three Gorges Dam Project.

RIGHT: A mountain waterfall in Wushan cascades down the sides of the gorge into the Yangtze River.

FAR LEFT: The world-famous Wu Gorge is one of the world-famous Three Gorges of the Yangtze.

LEFT: The Three Gorges dam spans the Yangtze River at Yichang. Originally conceived by Sun Yatsen in 1919 After final approval in April 1992, construction began in 1994 and reservoir began filling in June 2003, occupy part of the scenic area, between the cities of Yichang, Hubei Fuling and Chongqin. Final structural work was finished on May 2006, some nine months ahead of schedule. The facts and figures of the finished project are staggering. The dam is made of concrete and is about 7,660 ft (2335 m) long and 616 ft (185 m) high. It is 377 ft (115 m) wide on the bottom and 131 ft (40 m) wide on top and holds back a body of water 575 ft (1175 m) deep. The whole project employed a quarter of a million workers and employed moved about (134 million cu m) of earth, used 989 cu feet (28 million cu m) of concrete and 463 thousand tons of steel. The reservoir itself is over 375 miles (600 km) long. Although several generators still have to be installed, and the dam is not expected to become fully operational until about 2009, the total generating capacity is expected to reach 22,500 MW and claim the title of the largest hydroelectric dam in the world. Throughout the Yangtze Gorges, more than 1,300 villages and over 150 towns and cities have by now disappeared beneath these waters, forcing at least 1.2 million people to relocate. In addition, thousands of sites of archaeological and architectural interest are affected-some moved physically, others vanished for good. Nevertheless, the dam's supporters believe that it brings huge benefits that far outweigh these drawbacks.

RIGHT: The specatular Qutang Gorge of the Yangtze near Fengjie.

OVER PAGE: An excursion boat cruises along the Qutang Gorge on the Yangtze at low water level.

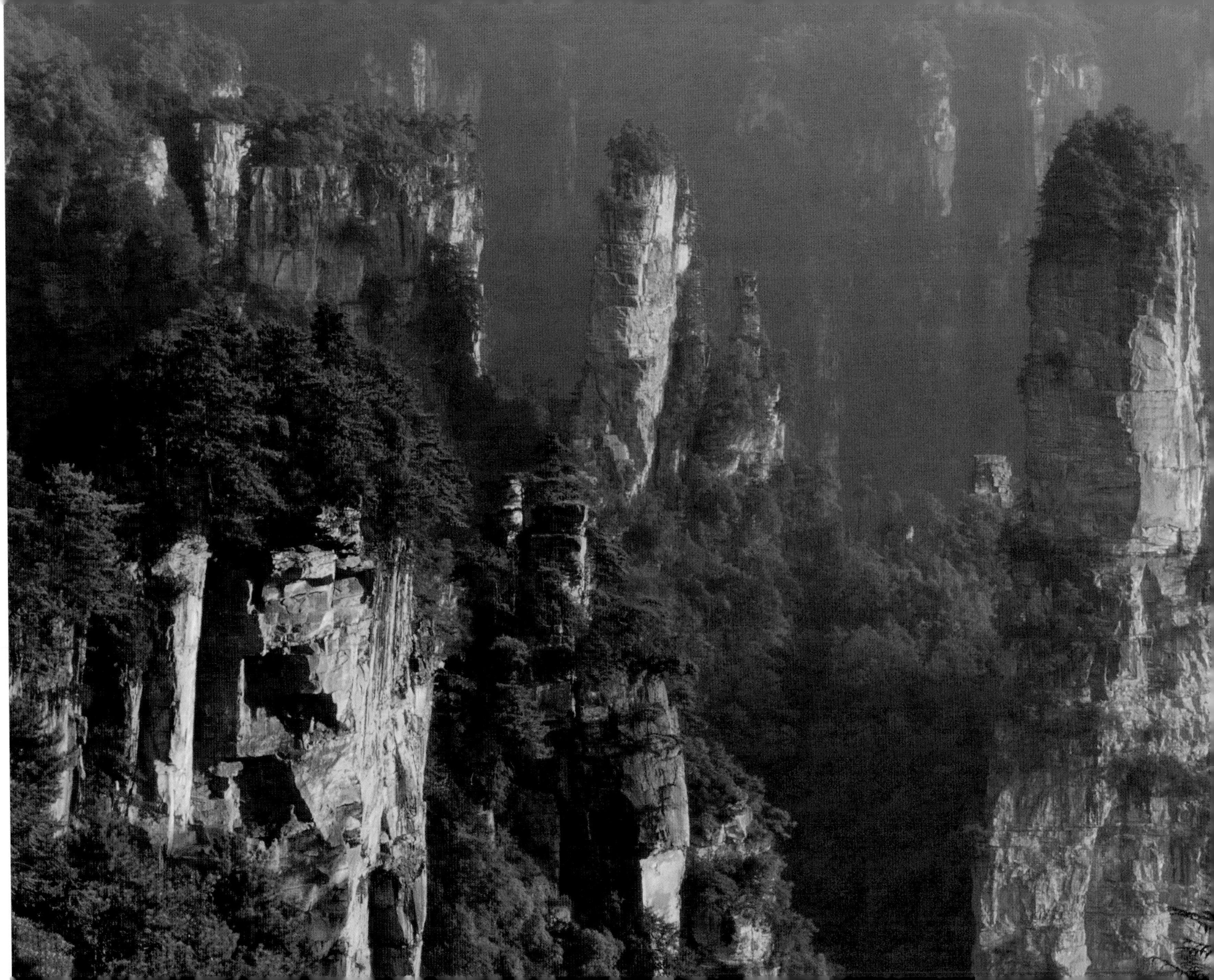

LEFT AND ABOVE: Zhangjiajie in Hunan was recognized as China's first National Forest Park in 1988 and in 1992 was officially recognized as a UNESCO World Natural Heritage site. The most notable geographic features of the park are the pillar-like formations that are seen throughout the park. Rising from the forest trees, they are the result of many years of erosion.

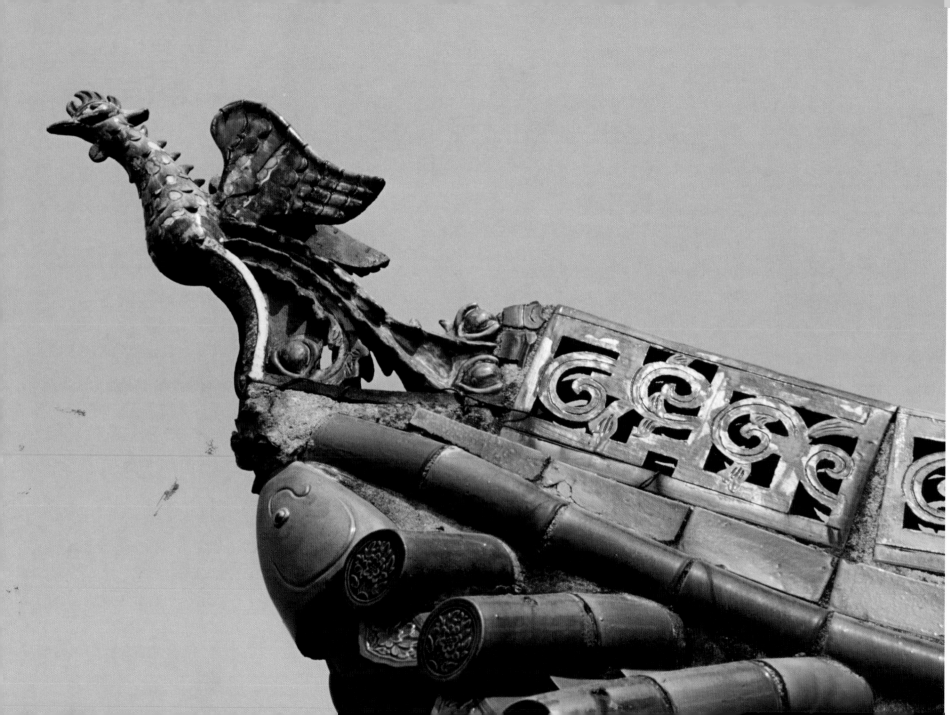

FAR LEFT: A beautifully carved bird statuette decorates the eaves of the Yueyang Temple, Hunan.

LEFT: Wulingyuan in Hunan is home to the three minority peoples, the Tujia, Miao and Bai, all of whom maintain their traditional cultures. It is also the location of the Zhangjiajie Scenic Area, a fascinating nature reserve that encompasses dramatic, mountain scenery rising subtropical rain forest-like this view from high up on the gorge of the upper Naren River.

ABOVE: A farmer leads her cattle along the riverbank beneath a bridge crossing the Yangtze. Many parts of Jiujiang, which is located on the southern side of the river, were largely devastated by flooding from the river in 1998 and massive efforts have been made since then to rebuild the river bank zone and flooded inner city areas.

OVER PAGE LEFT: A traditional crossing of the Gan River in Jiangxi consisting of a bridge supported by long row of small boats.

OVER PAGE RIGHT: Sunrise over a traditional style bridge at West Lake in Hangzhou, Zheijiang.

LEFT: Other parts of the West Lake shoreline are adorned with a vivid display of flowers.

RIGHT: Later in the morning, West Lake's pagodas provide a tranquil place in which to exercise.

SOUTHWEST CHINA

SOUTHWEST CHINA

Southwest China consists of the six provinces of Chongqing, Guangdongg, Guangxi, Guizhou, Hainan, and Yunnan as well as two former European colonies of Honk Kong and Macua, with their own special status. The provinces have a total land area of about half a million sq miles (1.2 million sq km) and a total population of around 243 million. The largest is Yunnan situated in the far southwest with an area of 394,000 sq km but it has a relatively small population of around 41.1 million. In contrast, Guangdongg covers an area of around 68, 710 sq miles (178,000 sq km) but is home to nearly 76 million people, mostly Cantonese-speakers. In absolute terms, the island of Hainan is the smallest at 13,125 sq miles (34,000 sq km) and least populated (8.2 million) of the provinces. Macua covers an area of just $10^1/_2$ sq miles (27.3 sq km) and around 450,000 people live there while larger Hong Kong has around 6.8 million residents.

The provincial capitals also vary in size enormously. Guangzhou, the capital of Guangdongg and one of China's richest urban areas, is home to 3.24 million people; while Guanxi's capital, Nanning, has just 1.3 million. Guiyang in Guizhou is equally small in Chinese terms, with some 1.7 million inhabitants. Haikou on Hainan, China's smallest and island province is the smallest of the southwest capitals with around 514,000 residents. The provincial government of Yunnan is based at Kunming in the northeast, a city with some 3.9 million residents.

Chongqing, although little known outside China, is likely to become home to one of the world's largest city, one with the same name that dominates the province. The city of Chongqing is already an economic giant, the major industrial center of the southwest, Furthermore, completion of the controversial Three Gorges Dam is likely to add to its industrial muscle by providing cheaper electricity and improved communications with Shanghai and Wuhan.

Guangdongg on the coast and close to Hong Kong had always benefited from international trade so that today it is the country's most prosperous provinces and much of the wealth is concentrated in Guangzhou itself.

In stark contrast Guangxi to the west is one of the country's poorest provinces partly due to its isolation and partly due to its geography but foreign-driven tourism is becoming of ever-greater importance. A major attraction is the Li River (or Li Jiang)–not to be confused with the Li (or Lishu) River in

PREVIOUS PAGES: The karst limestone heights and verdant valleys of Guangxi are characteristic of this part of China.

RIGHT: The Restoration Pagoda stands on the shores of Cheng-Ching Lake, a recreation area near Kaohsiung in Taiwan. Sculptures of deities adorn the pagoda roofs of the temple.

FAR RIGHT ABOVE: In a spectular, almost artistically-created pattern, more the 500 Taiwanese taxi drivers parked together to show their support for President Chen Shui-bian during a March 2006 election campaign rally in southern Kaohsiung.

FAR RIGHT BELOW: An impressive 14,603 tai chi enthusiasts managed to set a world record for the largest demonstration of the ancient Chinese martial art exercise method. It took place in front of the National Theater at Memorial Hall Park in Taipei on 23 November 2003.

Hunan that is one of the Yangtze's four largest tributaries in the province– rises in the Mao'er Mountains of Guangxi's Xingjian county and flows past the cities of Guilin and Yangshuo, form where cruises show tourist parties the stunning scenery and traditional life of the river.

Guizhou, Guanxi's neighbor to the southeast, is equally impoverished and the average income is something like a tenth of that of Shanghai. The authorities have undertaken a series of infrastructure projects to improve the province's links with the outside world and generate more tourist revenue, but there is a long way to go.

Hainan has achieved what Guizhou desires and today some 80% of the income of this once quite backwater is derived from tourism. The island is fringed by the golden beaches sought by its many tourists, but its interior is dominated by the forested uplands of the Limuling Shan.

Both Hong Kong and Macua were in foreign hands for many decades. Macua was formally occupied by the Portuguese in 1557 and finally returned to China in 1999, whereupon it was designated a Special Administrative Region. Macua, which currently covers just less than $10^1/_2$ sq miles (27 sq km), was built upon foreign trade, but this was later supported by income derived from thriving casinos but Macua remains something of an economic backwater and certainly lacks the financial muscle of near-neighbor Hong Kong, some 65 km to the east.

The latter was formally taken over by the British in the 1860s and a 99-year lease was signed in 1898. Thus Britain remained in control of Hong Kong until 1997, when it was returned to China. Hong Kong was built on trade between Europe and China, and one of the chief British exports into China was opium, a highly addictive drug the Chinese authorities were unable to prevent from entering the country despite their best efforts. The trade in opium has long gone, but Hong Kong remains a major port through which good are imported and exported into China. It has also emerged as the main financial center of the Far East and tourism, originally non-Chinese but increasingly from the mainland, is also a major contributor to the local economy.

Mountainous Chongqing is divided by the Yangtze, which flows from southwest to northeast through its central region and creates numerous steep-sided gorges. Guangdongg has also been largely defined by water as the Pearl River flows through the province before emptying into the South China Sea. But it also has mountain ranges, such as the Dayu Ling.

Guangxi, which translated as "vast, boundless west". It also boasts areas of beautiful limestone scenery and much of the province consists of mountainous zones dissected by rivers. Tourism is concentrated in the area around the stunningly beautiful village of Yangshuo.

In many ways, Guizhou is similar to Guangxi, as it has areas of limestone scenery but it also has mountains dotted with agricultural terraces and dense forests.

Yunnan is seen as one of the country most isolated province, one avoided by the mass tourism industry. Yet, it is probably one of China's most

diverse areas by any set of criteria. The terrain varies from tropical rainforest to mountains in the far north that are often covered in snow. Although Yunnan is somewhat isolated, it has benefited from some tourism around Lijiang and Xishuangbana. It is also developing an industrial base, especially around Kunming. Thanks, in part, to improvements in communications with the outside world, this city now boasts a variety of enterprises, including light engineering, plastics and textiles plants.

Southwest China contains the greatest concentrations of the country's various ethnic minorities. For example, some 75% of the people living in Guangxi are not Han Chinese but represent a mosaic of different groups, including the 15 million Zhuang as well as smaller groups of Dong, Maonan, Mulao, Jing, and Yi. Guizhou is equally rich in its human diversity with around 35% of its inhabitants coming from 18 different ethnic groups. Chief among these are the Dong and Ming. However, it is Yunnan that is home to a third of all of the country's ethnic minorities and roughly 35% of the province's peoples describe themselves as non-Chinese. Macua also exhibits some ethnic diversity–although the vast major are Chinese (95%), there are also Portuguese (2%) and Macanese (3%), peoples of mixed African, Chinese, and Portuguese ancestry.

LEFT: Being an island, the sea is never all that far away in Taiwan. These tidally-eroded, coastal rock formations are at Yehliu.

RIGHT: At the Chiang Kaishek Memorial in Taipei, the Gate of Great Centrality and Perfect Uprightness is surrounded by bright red flowers. Chang Kaishek was the military and political leader who assumed the headship of the Kuomingtang after the 1925 death of Sun Yatsen and who then led the national government of Taiwan.

LEFT: Taipei's East Gate, illuminated and decorated for a national holiday.

RIGHT: Taipei's night skyline, showing Taipei 101, the world's newest tallest building in 2004, standing at 1,671 feet (some 506 m) and with 101 floors. Designed by C. Y. Lee & Partners, the building is intended to reflect the nature of bamboo and embraces feng shui design, as well as the Chinese lucky number 8, their being eight separate pods of floors and eight autonomous floors within in each pod.

OVER PAGE LEFT: Taiwan's twin Dragon and Tiger pagodas at Kaohsiung, taiwan's second largest city.

OVER PAGE RIGHT: Nine Cornered Bridge and Wuli Pagoda at Kaohsiung

LEFT: The lower-than-normal water levels of the Yangtze River. A lasting drought has reduced the water in the Yangtze dramatically over the past month, severely cutting the local water supply in places like Chonqing City. This is especially crucial for the booming city, one of the fastest growing metropolises in the world and-as its third largest city-a symbol of modern China's industrial expansion.

RIGHT: Elsewhere in Chongqin, Buddhist cave sculpture created during the late Tang Dynasty through the Song Dynasty (9th century to 13th century) are a treasured vsitor attraction at Longgang in Dazu.

LEFT: Traffic moves along Jiablin Street in the Lowu district of central Shenzhen City, Guangdong. with the new office and apartment blocks that are now located there (**RIGHT**).

THIS PICTURE: Another high-rise building in Shenzhen, this time at Haiwang Plaza in the Nanshan district of the city. The modern architecture has been enhanced by this traditional sculpture of a horse.

LEFT: In another part of Shenzhen is the busy expressway intersection near the Capital Plaza Hotel, the white-and-blue stepped building seen at the far left.

RIGHT: Dusk falling over Hong Kong Island, seen form Victoria Peak and looking over the Mid-Levels skyscrapers to the Central District, Hong Kong Harbour and the Kowloon shore. Specifically, the buildings are The Centre, Two International Finance Centre ("Two IFC" and the tallest in Hong Kong), the Cheung Kong Centre and the Bank of China, with the Admiralty to the right.

FAR LEFT: Two IFC in the central District is Hong Kong's tallest building and is also (currently) the world's third highest.

LEFT: In this view across Charter Road from Statue Square, Hong Hong's architecture can be seen to be nothing if not one of contrasting styles and different eras. The glass edifice of the Bank of China rises on the left above the old courthouse building of colonial times and to the right is another glass tower, the Cheung Centre soaring above the white stone of the previous Bank of China building.

ABOVE: The late Kung Fu movie star Bruce Lee remains a hero in China as well as being of word renown. This bronze statute of him stands in tribute against the Hong Kong Island skyline on the Avenue of Stars, part of Kowloon's waterfront.

RIGHT: With modern protective covering but utilizing traditional bamboo scaffolding, the Hanoi Road project under construction, in January 2007, in the Tsim Sha Tsui district of Kowloon, Hong Kong.

LEFT: A reminder of Hong Kong's colonial past and architectural heritage of that era, The Old Clock Tower still stands on the Sha Tsui waterfront promenade section of Nathan Road in Kowloon.

RIGHT: Looking across Victoria Harbour from Kowloon, the Central District of Hong Kong Island's night skyline is graphically displayed with its impressive Christmas 2006 laser light show.

OVER PAGE LEFT: Victoria Harbour is one of the world's busiest and its traffic includes many ferries between Hong Kong Island, Kowloon, Lantau and the Lamma Islands. Among these are still the traditional boats that offer an effective water taxi service-contrasting with the daily business of the modern container ships berthed in the New Yau Ma Tei Typhoon Shelter beside Union Square in West Kowloon.

OVER PAGE RIGHT: The nightly display of almost garish neon signs in Kowloon.

RIGHT: The 135-feet (41-m) wide Tsing Ma Bridge is so named as it links the islands of Tsing-Yi and Ma-Wan on the Hong Kong peninsula. It has two decks and carries both road and rail traffic, which also makes it the largest suspension bridge of this type. The upper deck carries a dual, three-lane carriageway, whilst on the lower deck are two rail tracks and a two-lane emergency and maintenance roadway.

LEFT: Macau's colonial past as a Portuguese enclave on mainland China is still apparent in much of its older architecture and can be seen here as Senate Square begins to light up at dusk.

RIGHT: The European architecture of St. Paul's Cathedral is another obvious link with Macau's Portuguese colonial heritage. This part of its historic cneter was made a designated UNESCO World Heritage site in 2005.

金碧
（1.2樓）
娛樂場
CASINO
羅浮宮
（4樓）

LEFT: As a Special Administrative Region (SAR) of China, Macau is allowed its own governance and economic policy. In 2006, it surpassed Las Vegas to become the world's largest gambling earner with 6.95 billion dollars revenue form that industry and having attracted over 22 million visitors, mainly from China itself.

LEFT: The modern economic success and financial status of Macau is probably even more apparent than its past and the Bank of China tower stands as the tallest in the business district.

ABOVE: Bicycle transportation of plastic bottles and containers for recycling in Haiku, the capital of China's southern island province of Hainan. With a fifth of the world's population, the amount of waste in China has become an enormous problem. A collaborative study showed that about half of all waste plastics are left uncollected or dumped in an uncontrolled manner on land, in rivers or in the sea. Recycling is therefore especially important in a geographically finite environment such as the island of Hainan.

OVER PAGE LEFT: Near Longshen, in Guangxi, a farmer tends his terraced rice fields in June.

OVER PAGE RIGHT: In Guiin, Guangxi, the terraced paddy fields in Longji that are seen here shrouded in fog, are carved out of the Longshen hills and have a history of more than 650 years.

PREVIOUS PAGES: Rice fields and karst mounds around Yangshuo village in Guilin, Guangxo.

LEFT: Yangshuo village in Guangxi lies in the famous limestone karst scenery of Guilin. Expeditions into the surrounding countryside are increasingly popular with tourists. The whole of this scenic and historically important region was awarded UNESCO World heritage status in 1992.

LEFT: Dawn on the Li River, Yangshuo.

RIGHT: Fishing on the Li River.

OVER PAGE LEFT: A woman sails a bamboo raft on the Li River near Yangshuo.

OVER PAGE RIGHT: More modern craft on the Li include cruising tour boats.

LEFT: Denuded slopes of the Yangtze, shown here in Yunnan, attest to years of clear-cutting and deforestation. The practice was a main cause of floods that have killed thousands of people along the river in the past decades.

ABOVE: This dancer in ethnic costume is walking down stone steps after an outdoor performance of "Impression Lijiang" on Jade Dragon Snow Mountain in Yunnan. Nearly 500 amateur performers from 10 ethnic minority groups took part in the $31 million production in 2006 by the acclaimed Chinese director Zhang Yimou

RIGHT: A Taoist priest from Lijiang.

LEFT: The popular tourist destination of Tiger Leaping Gorge (or Hu Tiao Xiao), amongst the foothills of the Himalayas near Daju in northern Yunnan, is where the Jinsha Jiang river cuts dramatically through the soft rocks. At one point in the middle of the river lies a hard piece of granite, which has eroded much more slowly than the surrounding rock. It rises out of the river, pushing the fast flowing water into spectacular white water rapids, making Tiger Leaping Gorge one of the longest, deepest and narrowest river gorges in the world.

LEFT: Water filled rice terraces at sunrise in Yunnan.

OVER PAGE: Jade Dragon Snow Mountain in Shanzidou, with its highest peak reaching approximately 18,360 feet (5560 m) is the southernmost glacier in the northern hemisphere, stretching 22 miles (35 km) and a width of 13 miles (20 km). Seen here at a distance of about nine miles (15 km) from Lijiang Old Town, the snow-covered, fog-enlaced mountain is said to resemble a jade dragon lying in the clouds-hence its name.

LEFT: The Plaza Gate in Kunming, chief city of Yunnan province. Located at the northern edge of the large lake, its year-round temperate weather has earned it the name of "Spring City."

RIGHT: The beautiful Black Dragon Pool is situated to Lijiang, home to the Naxi minority people of Yunnan. The old town has survived virtually intact for some two hundred years, with its picturesque maze of cobbled streets, exquisite old wooden buildings, gushing canals and lively markets.

ABOVE: China has its own wineries and viniculture, as can be seen here in the rows of newly planted vines at the Yunnan Red Wine Winery.

RIGHT: Almost like a modern piece of art, this farmland of green winter wheat and red soil in the mountains is in the north of Yunnan.

FAR RIGHT: A patchwork of fields near Lijiang. The old city of Lijiang itself, being one of Yunnan's treasures, was given UNESCO World Heritage status in 1997.

ABOVE: Girls of the Jinuo people in Xishuangbanna wearing their traditional costume. Xishuangbanna lies on the border of China with Laos and Myanmar (Burma). It is a region of lush rainforest and subtropical weather, as well as being home to many of Yunnan's ethnic minorities like the Jinuo. It is increasingly popular with tourists, yet it is easy to get away from the crowds and experience everyday life in the countryside and villages.

RIGHT: A much younger Jinuo girl wears a traditional outfit during dance rehearsals for the Te Mao Ke ("Happy New Year") Festival in a village in the Jinuo Mountains. Natives of Xishuangbanna in the southern Chinese province of Yunnan, the people of the Jinuo ethnic group were the last group to be recognized as such by the Chinese government in 1979. Today, they are a population of just over 18,000.

THIS PAGE: Xishuangbanna in Yunnan is home to the Sanchahe Nature Reserve, its climate having created a unique area of dense jungle and rain forest. That same climate has also made an area of successful human cultivation. Here, Xishuangbanna farmers first plant rice seedlings in a flooded field and then work these resulting paddies with water buffalo. Later, the harvested rice is these and the grains dried, often still in the traditional way on smaller farms.

Illustration credits

Map on page 7 by Mark Franklin

Photographs on pages as listed courtesy of the sources listed below.

David Lyons
4, 14-15, 84, 85. 87, 88, 89, 90, 91, 140–147, 150–154. 160-161,166–169, 214–222.

Getty Images
Aurora: 133
Aurora/John Lee: 178-9
Axiom: 251
Bridgeman Art Library: 130
China Span: 12, 40, 43, 194, 195
DAJ: 8
De Agostini Picture Library: 129
Dorling Kindersley: 196
Getty Bank: 27 & 39
Hemis.fr: 232-3
Lonely Planet 41
Minden Pictures: 26 & 83
National Geographic: 52-3, 100 & 184
NGS: 97
Panoramics: 2-3, 64-5, 182-4
Photographer's Choice: 17, 51, 165(l) &186-7
Reportage: 79 &102
Robert Harding: 80-1, 82 & 230
Stone: 44-45, 49, 50
Taxi: 101

Corbis
Adrian Bradshaw: 197(r)
Alison Wright: 9, 110, 118-119 & 126-7
Arcaid/Greg Girard: 224
Arne Hodalic: 185
Bel Ombra/Jean Pierre Armet: 156l
Bob Krist: 128
Bob Sacha: 197(l) & 242
Bohemian Nomad Picturemakers: 66, 139(r) & 214
Brian A. Vikander: 116
Carl & Ann Purcell: 67 & 254-4
Christophe Boisvieux: 16, 158, 173(l), 175(l), 176, 243(r), 246-7 & 249
Craig Lovell: 94-5, 112-3 & 120

Dave Bartruff: 137
Dean Conger: 91 & 174
Diego Azubel/epa: 253(r)
Earl & Nazima Kowall: 44
Ed Kashi: 96
Epa: 24
Epa/Michael Reynolds: 78 &105(r)
Epa/Qi Zi: 78
Epa/Qiu Shafeng: 212
Eurasia Press/Steven Vidler: 111, 210 & 211
Eye Ubiquitous/Bennett Dean: 92(l)
Eye Ubiquitous/James Davis: 92(r)

Eye Ubiquitous/Julia Waterlow: 114(l & r) & 234
Frank Lukasseck: 154-5
Free Agents Limited: 208
Free Agents Limited/Dallas & John Heaton: 62, & 236-7
Galen Rowell: 117
JAI/Demetrio Carrasco: 148, 159, 170, 172
JAI/Michael Falzone: 114-5, 124
JAI/Neil Farrin: 223, 225
James Sparshatt: 63
Jason Lee/Reuters: 243(l)

John T. Young: 139(l)
Jon Hicks: 229(l)
Jose Fuste Raga: 33, 36, 37 38, 54, 59 68, 69, 70, 71, 72, 106, 107, 108, 109 181, 207, 238, 2148, 252 & 24-35
Kazuyoshi Nomachi: 121, 122 & 198
Keren Su: 1, 18, 98, 99t, 103, 104, 105(l), 157, 164, 165(r), 173(tr), 235, 240-1, 245, 250(r), 253(l), 255 & 256
Liu Liqun: 156(r); 162, 171(l & r), 175®
Louie Psihoyos: 5 & 209
Lowell Georgia: 149 & 163
Matthieu Paley: 20-1 & 22-3,

Michael S. Yamashita: 73 &138
Michel Setboun: 226
Mike Kemp: 244
Milepost: 92, 46 & 47
NASA: 77
Pablo San Juan; 19
Paul Souders: 180
Pierre Colombel: 173(br)
Reuters/China Photo: 229(r)
Redlink: 10-11, 13, 28-29, 30, 48, 55, 56-57, 177, 231 & 250(l)
Reuters/Nir Elias: 99(b)
Reuters/Simon Kwong: 205(rt & rb)

Ric Ergenbright: 32
Rick Friedman: 228
Robert Harding World Imagery/Tony Waltham: 25 & 131
Robert Harding/Charles Bowman: 227
Robert Harding/Christian Kober: 206
Robert van der Hilst: 58
Steven Vidler/Eurasia Press: 31, 200, 201, 213 & 239
Tibor Bognár: 199
Zefa/Bruno Levy: 125
Zefa/Frans Lemmens: 60 & 61
Zefa/Serge Kozak: 132

LEFT: These days, young Buddhist monks cannot avoid their traditional religious ways of life being impinged upon by the modern world, the wooden pagoda contrasting with the tailgate of a pickup truck.